M000283372

Advance Praise for
Don't Get Mad at Penguins

"Healthy conflict and extreme candor are crucial elements of communication in high-trust teams. Businesses with strong cultures, who embrace the teachings in this book, will grow faster and go further."

— Jay Farner, Vice-Chairman and
CEO of Rocket Companies

"*Don't Get Mad at Penguins* is a must read for anyone looking to thrive in today›s environment. It›s almost impossible to get ahead without learning how to navigate different personalities and manage the inherent conflict that exists when humans interact. Gabe provides a litany of useful tools and lessons that are essential to success."

— Eric Lefkofsky, Founder and CEO of Tempus;
Co-Founder and Chairman of Groupon

"*Don't Get Mad at Penguins* is entertaining and fun to read. Through captivating and inspiring stories, Gabe Karp shares invaluable lessons for detoxing conflict to lead a more successful, fulfilling, and happy life. Now that I'm armed with an entirely new skillset, I'm looking forward to my next conflict—and this time I'm ready!"

— Andy Friedman, Founder and
former CEO, SkinnyPop Popcorn

"Gabe may be a genius. Like Matt Damon in *Good Will Hunting*. When it comes to driving results through unprecedented and really cool techniques Gabe can 'just play.' We had very few rules at our companies. 'No yawning' and 'no sorries' were developed by our team. But, 'open communication solves all problems' was all Gabe. In *Don't Get Mad at Penguins*, Gabe winds us through a fun and notable path to conflict resolution that you will love. Guessing you'll read it twice. And, I didn't find a single spelling error."

— Robert Wolfe, Founder and former
CEO of Moosejaw and CrowdRise

"Business building is impossible without conflict and the more effectively we drive through conflict, the faster we build. Adherence to the lessons in *Don't Get Mad at Penguins* should put every leader on the path to success."

— Jason Raznick, Founder and Chief Zinger at
Benzinga, and a 2021 E&Y Entrepreneur of the Year

DON'T GET MAD AT PENGUINS

And Other Ways to Detox the Conflict
in Your Life and Business

GABE KARP

Post Hill
PRESS

A POST HILL PRESS BOOK
ISBN: 978-1-63758-163-6
ISBN (eBook): 978-1-63758-164-3

Don't Get Mad at Penguins:
And Other Ways to Detox the Conflict in Your Life and Business
© 2022 by Gabe Karp
All Rights Reserved

Cover design by Tiffani Shea

Although every effort has been made to ensure that the personal and professional advice present within this book is useful and appropriate, the author and publisher do not assume and hereby disclaim any liability to any person, business, or organization choosing to employ the guidance offered in this book.

No part of this book may be reproduced, stored in a retrieval system, or transmitted by any means without the written permission of the author and publisher.

Post Hill Press
New York • Nashville
posthillpress.com

Published in the United States of America
1 2 3 4 5 6 7 8 9 10

TABLE OF CONTENTS

INTRODUCTION

"**G**abe Karp, you look like shit," Steve grinned as he swept into the waiting area. His bold remark caught me off guard. To be fair, I was coming off of an exhausting red eye flight.

"Nice to meet you, too." I shook his hand.

I was here to observe Steve's company—let's call it Vulcan Solutions—because it had the fastest rate of growth *and* the highest level of conflict out of any company in my dataset. On the surface, their business model was boring (they manufacture recyclable synthetic rubber for medical devices). But under that conservative facade, this company was buzzing with confrontation during every meeting and, somehow, this confrontational culture was working well for them. I wanted to get to the bottom of what they were doing, so I asked their CEO, Steve, to let me shadow him for a day. What I saw during that visit completely contradicts how most people think conflict works.

While most of us generally fear and avoid conflict, it's a powerful asset for those who understand it. In fact, healthy conflict has been the greatest factor driving my success as a lawyer, entrepreneur, and venture capitalist. I wrote this book to help others benefit from conflict in the same way.

Of course, not *all* conflict is productive. There is healthy conflict, and there is toxic conflict.

While healthy conflict propels people and organizations forward, toxic conflict slows us down and causes pain. It consumes an organization's energy, taxing its ability to compete, grow, and prosper. When conflict turns toxic, team engagements are painful, client relationships are strained, and individual careers suffer. The same painful dynamics play out in our personal lives as well. Toxic conflict deprives us of the love, friendships, and relationships that we seek and need.

Toxic conflict, however, is far from inevitable. Just as we might go on a dietary cleanse to rid our bodies of toxins, we can do the same to detox our organizations and our minds—and when we do, the results are phenomenal. Once we cleanse the toxins, we suddenly feel energized to embrace conflict and leverage it to drive new innovation. We navigate difficult situations with ease and elevate our relationships to a higher plane. Detoxing our companies and our minds makes us better, stronger, faster, and more connected.

The path that led me to this perspective began when I was a trial lawyer investigating the sources of conflict in my cases. I had a front row seat to the conflicts of others, and I observed how certain communication styles always seemed to either improve or worsen a situation. In those days, a big part of my job was to control the level of conflict. During tense negotiations, I defused the conflict to help everyone relax and trust one another. During contentious cross-examinations, on the other hand, I amped up the tension when I wanted to rattle a witness or make a dramatic point to the jury.

While I served my clients well and achieved great results, I also suffered painful losses and struggled in difficult interactions with others for reasons I did not understand. Over time, I noticed the same patterns of conflict I'd seen in my cases play out in my personal life too. I was identifying the toxins that build up in human interactions and make them unhealthy. When my clients and I were able to detox those interactions, we were successful in resolving the conflicts. But when the toxins were left unchecked, we were generally in for an expensive and painful experience.

When I joined a small startup called ePrize and saw these same toxic patterns play out in the business world, I knew I was onto something important. Building a company from the ground up requires a lot of conflict. But I noticed that when we detoxed those conflicts, they really propelled our business forward. When we engaged in non-toxic confrontations with employees, clients, and shareholders, we achieved far superior results than when we avoided difficult issues or allowed toxins to infect interactions. This approach helped us grow our company into the world leader in the digital promotions industry. We acquired several smaller companies along the way and ultimately negotiated the sale of ePrize.

After our successful acquisition I entered the world of venture capital, where I've continued to experience the role of conflict on a broader scale. I have led the investments in and served on the board of directors of over a dozen companies, and I continue to witness the effects of both healthy and toxic conflict. I have negotiated business and financing deals in the hundreds of millions of dollars, and I've worked with CEOs to resolve conflicts ranging from clients wanting to cancel multi-million-dollar contracts to underperforming team members requesting pay raises, and everything in between. Regardless of how big or small the conflict, the same patterns play out over and over.

I've also seen the role that toxic conflict plays in the personal lives of the people I've worked with and those close to me. Sadly, I know people who no longer speak to each other because of political arguments on social media. Friends have confided in me about strained relationships with their parents, disputes with their neighbors, and challenges with their kids. The same patterns of conflict I saw in the business world apply in all walks of life (my own included).

Whether you're in the courtroom, the boardroom, the breakroom, a bar, the high school cafeteria, a parent-teacher conference, your holiday dinner table, or anywhere else humans interact, conflicts follow the same patterns. We all want to be better at managing conflict, but many of us never learned how. There's no class in school for it. Think about it: we spend months in elementary school learning long division, which we never use. Yet we spend zero time learning conflict management, something we all could use virtually every day.

The good news is that I've discovered a systematic way to detox conflict. It's a process I've developed through years of practical experience and academic research into how we can harness conflict to lead happier and more productive lives. Once I started to apply what I'd learned, I noticed immediate and dramatic improvements in my ability to successfully navigate conflict.

I realized I was onto something with these strategies a few years back when I was asked to speak to a group of CEOs about how to handle conflict. The speech was all right, but not my greatest. In the weeks and months that followed, though, I was approached by several of the CEOs and they all mentioned one of the ideas I had shared, especially one in particular: something called *Don't Get Mad at Penguins Because They Can't Fly*. I also received a strong positive reaction for a tactic I call the *Shopping List Voice* (which you'll read about later).

As I shared these tactics with others, many reported similarly positive results. So I researched and developed more strategies as well, teaching them to others and getting feedback. I've given presentations on conflict to companies, trade organizations, entrepreneur groups, lawyers, and universities, and I have received enough feedback on my approaches to know they are reliable and repeatable. These are skills anyone can learn and apply.

While some of us may fear conflict and others may love a good fight, we all have the ability to manage conflict to drive better outcomes for our companies, clients, and loved ones. The pages ahead will take you deep into the causes of conflict and provide you with tools to detox and leverage it for success and happiness.

A lack of understanding of how conflict works can explain why some companies rise and others fall—and why some careers are spectacular while others are tragic let-downs. By understanding the nature of conflict and how it can become toxic, we can rise above these challenges.

The real magic happens in organizations where conflict is not only accepted, but encouraged and required. These companies, families, and groups operate with candor and accountability. They execute at awe-inspiring speeds and blow past those who shy away from difficult issues. People within these special organizations communicate openly and clearly. They engage in free expression of ideas. Anyone with something to say has the opportunity to say it. Mistakes are uncovered quickly and performance issues are addressed without drama. People advance in their careers and grow in their personal lives in ways not possible when conflict is viewed as a negative.

Once you experience the benefits of non-toxic conflict, you will start to lean into it. You will invite it into your professional and personal life, and you'll use it to deepen your relationships and push your performance to the next level.

This book fills in the gaps left by the school system. It breaks down the factors that escalate conflict to dangerous heights and shows you how to defuse them and make conflict work *for* you, rather than *against* you. It will increase your empathy toward others, teach you to identify conflict traps before you fall into them, and help you view conflict as a productive driver of success. You'll learn simple but highly effective tools to embrace conflict so that it can fuel progress and help you communicate more effectively in all areas of life.

Along the way, you'll see the fight that ended Quentin Tarantino and Uma Thurman's friendship; the swear words that were accidentally printed on thousands of Pampers diapers packages; the toxic culture at General Motors that cost the company over $2 billion and killed 124 people; and the inner workings of Seal Team 6, the elite crew that took out Osama bin Laden. You'll also meet the Buddhist monk who saved thousands from child prostitution because he was willing to treat the leaders of a Beijing crime syndicate like human beings; the executive who sues people for sport; the judge who made me feel good even as he ruled against me; and the woman who ended a years-long cycle of personal conflict with her ex-husband once she learned to stop getting mad at penguins. I've changed some names and settings to protect identities, but the substance and lessons of these stories remain intact.

Before we can get to all of that, however, I have to tell you what happened at Vulcan Solutions when I went to shadow Steve for the day and observe his completely unorthodox style of conflict management....

CHAPTER 1

To Embrace or Resist Conflict?

In researching this book, I analyzed data from over one hundred sources to determine the ideal level of conflict in an organization. I assumed I already knew the answer before I started: some conflict is beneficial, but you don't want to have too much of it, or too little. Ignoring conflict isn't healthy, I figured, but dwelling on past disagreements isn't productive either. The most effective approach, I thought, would be somewhere in between.

However, the results told a different story. I found that the more conflict a company had among team members, the faster it tended to grow. From the look of things, conflict was a *good* thing. But there was an important caveat: this was only true for companies where the employees maintained strong, trusting relationships in spite of high levels of conflict.

That finding was what sent me to the headquarters of Vulcan Solutions to shadow Steve, the CEO, for the day. His company simultaneously had the highest level of conflict *and* the fastest rate of growth in my entire dataset. What were they doing here that was so special?

I bounded after Steve as he slipped through a side door and down a narrow corridor on the way to our first meeting. Then we stepped into a conference room, where Steve introduced me to a man and a woman. "This is Gabe," he announced, winking at me. "I'm training him to handle conflict in the workplace." The other two were vice presidents in the design and fabrication departments, and Steve was there to review their quarterly progress. I've sat in hundreds of these meetings during my years as an executive and as a board member.

But that couldn't have prepared me for what I was about to see.

The conflict started immediately when a VP didn't know the answer to one of Steve's questions. "Stacey is working on that," she said. "Let me check with her."

Then, a few minutes later, the other VP made a similar statement: "I'm not sure on those exact numbers," he said. "Stacey has those and I can get them from her."

And then, less than five minutes after that, it happened again: "I'll grab those exact details from Stacey."

"I need to ask a question," Steve said, puzzled. "Who the fuck is Stacey?"

"We hired her a few months ago," came the reply. "She's doing great, especially since she's only twenty-three, and we recruited her straight out of college with no manufacturing experience."

"That's the third time in this meeting that one of you has said you need to check with Stacey on something." Steve didn't yell, but he spoke with an intensity that commanded the room. "Next time that happens, I'm giving Stacey a $10,000 raise. And if it happens again, I'm giving her another $10,000 raise. And if I start to pay Stacey that much money for doing *your* work, then what the fuck do I need you for?"

The VPs were silent.

"Should we reconvene in an hour so you can go have Stacey teach you what the fuck is going on?" Steve asked, his voice calm. "Because otherwise, Stacey should be sitting here instead of you." As a side note, Steve's f-bomb-to-total-word ratio is one of the highest I've ever seen.

Slowly, the VPs nodded their heads. Then they apologized to Steve and promised to do better in the future.

"You're right," one VP said. "We haven't been as involved as we should be on this, and Stacey has really been picking up the slack."

"We'll take care of it," said the other VP. "Thanks for pointing it out. You're absolutely right."

The two of them packed up their things and filed out of the room—and Steve and I headed off to his next meeting of the day. It played out in much the same way, with Steve giving harsh and blunt feedback to the employees about their performance and them thanking him and promising to work on his suggestions going forward.

Every meeting at Vulcan Solutions followed a similar script. Steve always asked thoughtful and probing questions before eventually saying some variation of "this is crap," but without getting angry or emotional. Despite Steve's harsh language, the meetings did not feel uncomfortable, and I did not get the sense from anyone that they felt disrespected or treated unfairly. Some people were obviously embarrassed, but everyone took full ownership of the issues when Steve pointed them out and seemed to immediately move forward to address them.

At most companies, executives work hard to position constructive criticisms between two pieces of praise (the classic "shit sandwich" approach), but employees still get upset about receiving feedback. Steve, on the other hand, says whatever is on his mind—cuss words and all—and doesn't rub anyone the wrong way. He has created a culture where no one shies away from direct feedback, and no one is offended when they receive it. In fact, brutal honesty is preferred by everyone.

Importantly, this is very much a two-way street at Vulcan. I saw Megan, a team leader, criticize Steve for telling one of her direct reports a few days earlier to drop what he was doing and help Steve with something. Megan said that particular team member was working on a time-sensitive project, and if Steve had come to her first, she would have gotten someone else to help him. She felt Steve undermined her authority, jeopardized missing an important deadline, and basically made her job harder. Megan didn't yell or complain; her tone was matter-of-fact.

Steve immediately responded, "I guess I did a pretty good job screwing that one up." He looked at her with sincerity and said, "I'm sorry. That was wrong of me. I'm going to apologize to your team member for pulling him off a project without checking with you first and tell him that if I ever do that again, he should feel free to ask if I've cleared it with you."

She smiled and said with a wink, "No problem. Just don't ever do it again."

The culture at Vulcan Solutions just *works*.

Unfortunately, this culture is the exception, not the rule. Many business cultures are engineered to avoid conflict. Mistakes are frowned upon and seen as badges of shame. Conformity takes priority over accountability. Surrounded by this toxic culture, many of us feel unsafe expressing contrary opinions.

Outside of work, the barrage of toxic conflict in social media and the news wears us down. We keep critical feedback to ourselves, afraid of offending a coworker (even when feedback would help the person improve). We are reluctant to call out problems or disagree with someone—especially an authority figure. *When in doubt, say nothing. Don't share any opinions or feedback that could make someone feel bad.* The well-intentioned desire to be respectful and polite has led to an environment in which people only say what they think others want to hear. This mentality deprives us of the opportunity to correct mistakes, improve behavior, and strive toward our maximum potential.

We all need candid feedback, and by censoring our comments to avoid ruffling feathers, we do a great disservice to one another. People who are able to accept direct feedback will learn and improve faster than those who can't. If helpful feedback is withheld from an employee because their boss is afraid to hurt their feelings, that boss has denied the employee a valuable opportunity to grow and improve. The boss's compassion is misdirected into silence instead of feedback, and the one who suffers is the employee. How's that for irony?

Looking out for people doesn't mean smiling, being nice, and telling them what they want to hear. It often requires giving difficult feedback to help them grow. In fact, it would be cruel and disrespectful to withhold that kind of feedback. But even though we all would benefit from a culture where candid communication is welcomed and encouraged, that kind of environment is rare and does not happen by chance.

Thankfully, even the most toxic environment can be detoxed. You can take a culture where unhealthy conflict is rampant and turn it into a place like Vulcan Solutions.

Mary Barra experienced the need to change a culture of unhealthy conflict firsthand when she took the helm at General Motors (GM) in the middle of one of the worst crises the company has ever faced. Sixteen days after becoming CEO on January 15, 2014, she learned GM had been installing defective ignition switches in its vehicles. Car accidents were occurring across the country, causing serious injuries and death. But this had been covered up at GM for years.

The first victim of GM's negligence was Amber Marie Rose, a sixteen-year-old who was driving her new Chevy Cobalt in the early morning hours of July 19, 2005, when it crashed into a tree outside of eastern Dentsville, South Carolina.[1] She died hours later at the hospital. An investigation revealed that a design flaw in the car's ignition had caused the vehicle to suddenly switch to the "accessory" position while Amber was driving. This shut off the engine and disengaged the safety systems, including the power steering, anti-lock brakes, and airbags.

---

1   Jensen, Christopher. "In General Motors Recalls, Inaction and Trail of Fatal Crashes." *The New York Times,* March 2, 2014. https://www. nytimes.com/2014/03/03/business/in-general-motors-recalls-inaction-and-trail-of-fatal-crashes.html. Accessed October 18, 2021.

But Amber's tragedy was only the beginning. The ignition switch defect ultimately caused 124 deaths and 275 injuries.[2] The financial impact to GM was devastating, leading to the recall of 30 million vehicles worldwide and costing GM over $2.5 billion in fines and settlements, not to mention the massive loss of trust of its customer base, its shareholders, and the public at large.[3]

Mary Barra discovered, to her horror, that GM had been attempting to avoid responsibility for the ignition switch problem. For example, five months after Amber's accident, GM had sent its dealers a bulletin stating that an ignition switch defect can occur when "*the driver is short and has a large and/or heavy key chain…the customer should be advised of this potential and should…[remove] unessential items from their key chain.*"[4] Let that sink in for a minute. GM knew its cars had a defect that could suddenly shut off the vehicle—disabling power steering, anti-lock brakes, and air bags—while the vehicle was traveling at high speeds, and the company's response was to suggest that people avoid big key chains, rather than to issue an immediate recall. Sadly, the tragedies continued.

---

2   LaReau, Jamie L. "GM: We encourage employees, dealers to tattle after ignition switch crisis." *Detroit Free Press*, September 6, 2019. https://www.freep.com/story/money/cars/general-motors/2019/09/06/gm-ignition-switch-nhtsa-recalls-safety-defects/2099289001/. Accessed October 18, 2021.

3   Ibid.

4   Basu, Tanya. "Timeline: A History Of GM's Ignition Switch Defect." NPR.org, March 31, 2014. https://www.npr.org/2014/03/31/297158876/timeline-a-history-of-gms-ignition-switch-defect. Accessed October 18, 2021.

To fix these problems, Barra realized she needed to embrace conflict head-on. She launched a thorough investigation and discovered the real problem wasn't an engineering issue. It was high levels of toxic conflict in the organization. She learned there were people within GM who had known for more than ten years about the faulty ignition switches, but had kept quiet out of fear they would be bullied, fired, harassed, and/or ridiculed. General Motors had a culture that discouraged employees from raising safety concerns.[5] While the design defect was a technical problem, the root cause was a cultural one.

In April of 2014, Barra appeared before Congress to speak about the ignition switch defect.[6] Instead of making excuses or shying away from the issues, she apologized for GM's past actions, acknowledged their deficits, and offered an honest explanation for why the company had been dragging its feet. She admitted the situation was GM's fault and assured the world that things were changing.

Under Barra's leadership, GM issued massive recalls of affected vehicles, provided unprecedented transparency to investigators, and stepped up to be held accountable for its behavior. She used the opportunity to reinvent the company

5   Valukas, Anton R. "Report to Board of Directors of General Motors Company Regarding Ignition Switch Recalls," 252–256. https://s3.documentcloud.org/documents/1183508/g-m-internal-investigation-report.pdf. Accessed October 18, 2021.

6   Mary Bara full testimony before U.S. House of Representatives, Oversight and Investigations Subcommittee. "The GM Ignition Switch Recall: Why Did It Take So Long?" April 1, 2014. C-Span.org. https://www.c-span.org/video/?318608-1/gm-ignition-switch-recall. Accessed October 18, 2021.

and its brand, to revamp the internal culture, and to reestablish trust with the public. Safety and customer focus became the center of every decision.

An example from 2019 demonstrates these results in action.[7] An assembly line worker at a GM plant noticed that a part appeared to be installed incorrectly. He submitted a "Speak Up" alert, and GM investigated immediately. Because of the early warning, GM had to repair fewer than 200 cars. Before Mary Barra changed the culture, that production defect likely would have gone unreported and affected tens of thousands of vehicles coming off that assembly line.

Mary Barra was able to detox GM's culture and her efforts paid off. Today, the company is performing at extraordinary levels, reaching new heights in shareholder value and profitability. All of this was possible because Mary Barra embraced conflict, managed it proactively, and leveraged it to drive progress. She used formal processes and policies to detox the culture at GM, whereas at Vulcan Solutions, the healthy culture of conflict flowed naturally from Steve's leadership and his brutally honest but non-threatening communication style. While these two approaches were very different, the results were the same. Both companies created environments that keep toxic conflict at bay.

Of course, toxic conflict isn't reserved just for the GMs of the world. We all experience conflict in a variety of forms

---

7   LaReau, Jamie L. "GM: We encourage employees, dealers to tattle after ignition switch crisis." *Detroit Free Press*, September 6, 2019. https://www.freep.com/story/money/cars/general-motors/2019/09/06/gm-ignition-switch-nhtsa-recalls-safety-defects/2099289001/. Accessed October 18, 2021.

every day. Even something as simple as a few harsh words or a critical facial expression can stir our emotions and affect us deeply. My mom still remembers the stinging feeling of humiliation when she was accused of shoplifting decades ago by a well-meaning security guard at the mall. She'd gone to the department store to exchange a onesie she'd bought for my brother a few days earlier. She simply needed a different size. It was mid-December, the peak of holiday shopping, and the store was busy and chaotic. She found the new onesie in the correct size and looked around for an associate to help with the exchange, but none was in sight. She checked the tags on both garments—the prices were identical. So she put the onesie she'd purchased a few days earlier on the table, grabbed the new one, and headed for the door.

She was almost out of the store when a security guard grabbed her arm with a firm hand and said, "Where do you think you're going?!" My mom's anxiety level shot into overwhelmed-mode and she meekly tried to explain the situation, but the security guard said, "That's a likely story," and took her to an interrogation room. Sitting there alone in *department store jail*, all she could think of was the shame this scandal would bring her family if anyone found out. About ten minutes later, the guard returned and said, "You can go now, but don't ever do anything like this again." The ordeal had shaken my mom. She dwelled on it for days, reliving the stress of the incident repeatedly in her mind.

Reflecting on it now, my mom wishes she'd simply stood up for herself, calmly explained the situation, showed the security guard the receipt, and left. But when conflict descended upon her without warning, it triggered a panicked emotional response and she shut down. (I'm sure it would have been even more harrowing if she weren't a suburban white woman.)

Even though the security guard used professional language, the encounter triggered my mom's fight-or-flight response. On the other hand, Steve's blunt, profanity-laced comments at Vulcan Solutions do not trigger any of his team members to get emotional. This illustrates how certain factors can detox an environment so that conflict proceeds in a healthy way.

While this department store incident is minor compared to the General Motors ignition switch tragedy, the same factors are at play. Just like those GM engineers who knew about the ignition switch defect for ten years but never came forward, my mom withdrew and kept silent in the face of conflict, and it ultimately made the situation worse. While these two scenarios might seem worlds apart on the surface, when we look deeper, the only difference between them is severity. All toxic conflicts follow a set of simple patterns, regardless of the scale, situation, or number of parties involved. And this means the same tools can be used to overcome a wide variety of highly charged interpersonal situations.

Before we can talk about how to overcome toxic conflict, it helps to understand where it comes from in the first place.

WHY IS CONFLICT SO HARD?

Like most human traits, conflict has its roots in both Nature and Nurture. The animal kingdom is rife with conflict; it is an indispensable feature of life. But humans take this to a whole new level. Whenever humans interact, there is conflict: between family and friends, employees and employers, and nations on the global stage. We even have the unique ability to engage in entirely internal conflicts, where we debate against ourselves inside of our own heads.

It's important to note that conflict in some form is inevitable. History books may paint human achievement as a clear progression from one feat, invention, or discovery to the next, but that progress takes place in the midst of adversity, dissent, and even violent opposition. Conflict is fundamental to life. Any worthwhile achievement involves overcoming resistance. The notion that conflict is bad and should be avoided is wrong and can be downright harmful. Trying to avoid conflict usually makes things worse, like it did for General Motors and for my mom at the shopping mall.

Let's look at the two main drivers of conflict in more detail. First, we'll explore the Nature component and see how our brains are wired to respond to conflict in certain ways from birth. Then we'll cover the Nurture side of things and see how our environment socializes us to deal with conflict in ways that can be counterproductive.

Survival Instinct

The first driver of toxic conflict is Nature, or our innate genetic predispositions, which work well to protect us from physical threats in the jungle but can backfire when applied to interpersonal dynamics. We all have over a billion years of evolution hard coded into our DNA and conflict can trigger our instinctive survival system, sending us into fight-or-flight mode. This system is really a set of reflexive responses that cause us to either lash out and escalate a conflict (fight) or shy away and withdraw (flight). If we allow these instincts get the better of us, our emotions will quickly reach toxic levels, leading to unhealthy conflict.

Our instinctive responses to conflict come from two almond-shaped glands in the brain called the amygdala, located behind the eyes and optic nerve. The amygdala first evolved around 200 million years ago in the brains of our prehistoric ancestors, and it is responsible for detecting threats and responding to emergencies. When we perceive a threat, the amygdala jumps into the driver's seat and takes over the controls from the slower-thinking, rational areas of our brains. The amygdala doesn't stop to think because in a life-or-death situation, every second counts. A cascade of stress hormones floods our system to get the body ready for one of two things: fight or flight. We may feel butterflies in our stomach, sweaty palms, and flushed cheeks. Our heart races; our limbs and voice feel shaky; the throat constricts; our neck tightens; and our breathing becomes rapid and shallow as we take in more oxygen for a surge of energy to either attack or run away.

When the amygdala goes into fight-or-flight mode, our brain shuts down the neural pathways to the prefrontal cortex, which is the seat of logic, reason, planning, and goal setting. That's the part of our brain that makes good decisions, figures out answers, and carefully weighs the consequences of our actions. A functioning prefrontal cortex is necessary when we want to reason and think deeply. But when we're threatened, there's no time for that. We're in survival mode: no thinking allowed, only action.

This works great during a *physical* conflict, but not during a verbal one.

Without access to our prefrontal cortex, we can become disoriented during heated conversations and lose the ability to consider multiple perspectives. Have you ever thought of the perfect response to a conflict hours after it ended? That's because access to your prefrontal cortex was shut down in the heat of the moment, and once it came back online you were able to process the interaction and think of a creative solution.

Our memories can also become untrustworthy in fight-or-flight mode. Have you ever been in an argument with a friend or loved one and been unable remember one positive thing about them? When we are triggered into fight-or-flight mode, we lose the ability to see things from someone else's point of view. Our focus narrows to a singular goal: *deal with this threat now*. We can't choose how to react because our genetically-bred nervous system does it for us. And all of this happens before our conscious mind even registers what's going on.

In the jungle, fight-or-flight responses save lives. But in the boardroom, classroom, or family room, these responses can cause serious problems. When our ancestors walked out of a cave and saw a saber-toothed tiger, their amygdalae kicked into high gear and protected them from the threat. There were others at the time who casually looked at the saber-toothed tiger and thought, *Cool.* They were not our ancestors. The official scientific term for guys like that is "lunch," and they didn't live long enough to pass their weak amygdala genes on to future generations. Back then, possessing a strong amygdala was a matter of life and death. But in today's world, where the type of threat we face is often a big test at school, an important presentation at work, or a politically-charged relative at a family gathering, our hair-trigger amygdala can get us into big trouble.

Survival emotions like fear and anger can be useful in resolving physically threatening situations. However, in nuanced encounters, these emotions quickly rise to toxic levels. Our amygdala thinks we're facing a saber-toothed tiger, not Shelly from accounting. Healthy conflict turns toxic. That's the first reason conflict is so difficult to manage.

Socialization

The second driver of toxic conflict has its roots in Nurture: we are influenced by the things we learn about conflict from our culture, family, and friends over the course of our lives. We are socialized from a young age to soften bad news and sugarcoat feedback. We're told, "If you don't have something nice to say, don't say anything at all." We are taught to be respectful, agreeable, and polite. Of course, those are important lessons, but this conditioning can make us feel it's rude to disagree with anyone about anything, which can ultimately make conflicts worse (like it did for GM and for my mom at the mall).

When it comes to fear and anger, we receive conflicting messages that condition us to be considerate while simultaneously being assertive. For example, society teaches boys and men that fear is a sign of weakness. Anger, however, is encouraged. Coaches in organized sports teach boys from an early age to "get angry" and channel that emotion toward competition. Authority figures remind boys to assert themselves and stand up to bullies. Women and girls, on the other hand, often receive exactly the opposite conditioning. Anger and aggressive behavior are discouraged and viewed as impolite, even "bitchy." At the same time, tactful and demure behavior is encouraged and praised. Girls are often warned away from doing anything that involves risk; they are taught to be afraid. These are certainly generalizations, and gender-based conditioning in western culture is changing, but the conflicting messages are there.

We are also socialized in conflicting ways when it comes to the two other critical conflict toxins: judgment and ego.

The judgment training starts early, and the messages we receive are confusing and contradictory. Kids are taught not to talk to strangers, which is a valuable lesson, but one that can engender a general distrust of others. At the same time, we are told not to judge people, and that we should accept others as they are. So...we should judge the creepy guy in the van but accept everyone else?

From an early age, we also receive conflicting messages about ego-driven behavior. Popular culture bombards us with messages of individual triumph and overcoming adversity.

The media celebrate bold heroes who stare down conflict and rise to challenges. We worship visionary thinkers who have the confidence to stand up to the herd and who dare to be different. But then again, we are taught to stay humble, and we learn to judge arrogance negatively.

All of these are valuable lessons and wise words to live by, but the contradictions created by these competing messages cause confusion that can lead us to miss the mark. One impact is that most of us have a tendency to act and react in ways that can create conflict where none existed, or to escalate a negative situation to make things even worse. In short, the second major problem is that our *socialization* can lead us into toxic conflict.

The Four Toxins

As a result of our Nature and Nurture, there are four toxins that create the majority of unhealthy conflict in our lives: fear, anger, judgment, and ego. Certainly, other emotions influence conflict too (jealousy, greed, lust, etc.), but I've found that focusing on these four crucial toxins yields life-changing benefits. Fear, anger, judgment, and ego are natural and healthy, and when they occur within optimal ranges, they drive us to resolve problems, neutralize threats, and stand up for ourselves. In safe ranges, these feelings can take many forms, including a sense of competition; a need to be seen and valued; or a desire to make productive contributions. However, when any of these four things gets too high or too low, they act as toxins, making our interactions unhealthy in the same way that toxins in our bodies make us physically unhealthy.

The goal is not to eliminate these four toxins from our lives completely, but to keep them at optimal levels, cleanse their toxic effects from our interactions, and engage conflict in positive ways that drive success and happiness.

Nearly every substance we consider to be healthy can also become toxic when its concentration in the body rises too high or drops too low. The human body works best in a state of homeostasis, meaning we need to keep everything within an optimal range in order to thrive. For instance, water is the most abundant molecule in the human body, making up approximately 60 percent of our weight.[8] Drink too little and you'll become dehydrated. Consume too much and you'll risk water poisoning, which can be fatal. The same is true for iron: too little results in anemia, while too much leads to hemochromatosis (which even sounds bad). Potassium follows the same pattern. So does sugar, cholesterol, zinc, vitamin E, and so on.

Conflict works in much the same way: when your emotions remain within optimal ranges, your interactions will be healthy. Allow these emotional levels to get too high or too low and their impact on conflict will be toxic.

Just as nutritionists focus their attention on optimizing your levels of a handful of critical vitamins and minerals, I've found that focusing on these four toxins will do wonders to promote healthy conflict. There are thousands of molecules known to influence human health, and new candidates are discovered all the time. It's impossible and unnecessary

---

8   Sissons, Claire. "What is the average percentage of water in the human body?" May 27, 2020. https://www.medicalnewstoday.com/articles/what-percentage-of-the-human-body-is-water. Accessed October 18, 2021.

to optimize all of them. The typical multivitamin contains around twenty to twenty-five different nutrients.

When it comes to conflict, it's even simpler. Focus on keeping fear, anger, judgment, and ego within optimal ranges. This will dramatically reduce toxic conflict in your life. Yes, there are certainly many other instincts and emotions that influence conflict, too, but keeping these four crucial factors from reaching toxic levels is the best place to start.

Fear

A healthy level of fear is essential to survival, but when fear gets out of its optimal range, the effects can be toxic. When we perceive a physical threat in our environment, fear can motivate us to neutralize it or run away, which is undoubtedly good. Similarly, if a situation at work threatens the promotion we want or places our job in jeopardy, fear can keep us vigilant and motivate us to take action. On the other hand, when we aren't scared enough during a conflict, bad things can happen. We might feel emboldened and rush into a trap, mouth off at the wrong time, or take something too far without stopping to think. But too much fear isn't productive either. It can cause us to avoid dealing with a threat, allowing it to grow into a greater one. It can lead us to run away from a fight, rather than standing up for ourselves with confidence. In order to detox our conflict, we must learn to keep fear within the optimal range.

Anger

Anger can be either healthy or toxic as well. I got this from a show on Netflix (*The Queen's Gambit*): *"Anger is a potent spice. A pinch wakes you up; too much dulls your senses."* In many ways, anger is helpful. When we experience a problem, frustration often motivates us to fix it rather than allowing it to fester. However, anger can also make us impulsive and irrational at a time when we need to be thoughtful and deliberate. Anger can cause us to lash out and alienate someone who might have helped us fix our problem. It can prevent us from considering options, seeing other perspectives, and working collaboratively toward solutions. There is an optimal amount of anger, but if we let this emotion rise too high or drop too low, the effects will be toxic.

Judgment

Just like fear and anger, judgment works best within a certain range. Some judgment is helpful, like when we steer clear of a dangerous situation because something doesn't feel right, or when we give a deserving person a second chance because we judge her to have good overall character. However, exercising too little judgment can lead to us being taken advantage of. And excessive judgment can close us off to hearing others out or exploring opportunities that might benefit us. Further, overt judgment that comes across in our communication can discourage people from engaging with us.

Ego

The final factor that can lead to toxic conflict unless we maintain it within an optimal range is ego. If someone undervalues us or tries to steal our ideas, it's a good thing for our ego to push us to make our contributions known. But ego can also drop or elevate to toxic levels that make conflict worse. Without enough ego, we can allow others to take credit away from us or ignore our value. Too much, however, can push us to make self-righteous statements that we later regret, or to take hasty actions with over-inflated, unwarranted confidence.

The fear, anger, judgments, and egos of the people we interact with can have just as much impact on conflict as our own. So, we should view these emotions not just from our own perspective, but from the objective perspective of conflict itself (technically, judgment and ego are not emotions, but I'm taking creative license for simplicity). We can proactively manage the emotions of others to prevent them from reaching toxic levels. By focusing on these toxins and working to keep them within optimal ranges, we can make conflict work *for* us rather than *against* us. But how?

CREATING AN ENVIRONMENT WITH HEALTHY CONFLICT

The good news is that we can overcome our Nature and Nurture to create an environment in which people are comfortable engaging in conflict without allowing it to turn toxic. There are simple, straightforward things we can do to neutralize these toxins. We can actively prevent anger, fear, judgment, and ego from reaching toxic levels that send us into fight-or-flight mode, and we can maintain access to the more sophisticated areas of our brain even in the most stressful situations. Once we learn how toxins build up, we can use specific tactics to steer clear of our survival emotions and detox our conflict. This isn't a special talent that only a privileged few are born with. This is a skill everyone can learn and improve upon.

I saw the power of these tactics firsthand on an organizational level when I was building the legal team at ePrize, a startup specializing in digital promotions for major brands. That team was responsible for ensuring that none of our promotions ran into legal trouble. My task was to train people without any legal experience to debate with lawyers, call out legal mistakes, and challenge one another's positions. But I quickly realized that many on the team, especially some who were in their very first job out of college, wouldn't challenge each other because they felt confrontation was impolite, disrespectful, and unprofessional. A team cannot be successful unless teammates regularly call out mistakes, challenge ideas, and debate issues. This was a serious problem. During team meetings, I implored my employees to challenge anything I said that didn't make sense. I explained that we didn't have the luxury of going along with something simply because everyone else seemed to agree. They would nod in agreement, but the culture wasn't changing.

One day, in a team meeting, we were trying to navigate a pesky problem and someone suggested a solution, but then asked whether it was legal. With a straight face, I name-dropped a completely made-up Supreme Court case with the most absurd facts and ridiculous ruling I could think of, hoping my team would challenge me. But everyone just accepted what I said without comment. I pushed the issue:

Me: Does that make sense to everyone?

Team: Not really. It kind of doesn't make sense at all.

Me: You're right. It sounds absolutely ridiculous. Why didn't you question it?

Team: Because you said it with such authority, we figured it must be correct.

Me: I completely made it up. Your instincts were spot on. If something doesn't sound right, you've got to question it, no matter where you hear it. You can't let anyone get away with saying something that doesn't make sense, especially me.

Once the team understood I was capable of making things up, their concerns over being impolite disappeared and it turned into a game. They questioned and challenged even the legitimate things I said, which was exactly what I wanted.

When I engaged their challenges in a nonconfrontational way, it removed their fear that conflict could turn negative. Soon they felt comfortable challenging one another's statements as well.

So, with a few made up court cases, we were able to make everyone comfortable challenging ideas, opinions, and suggestions without fear that the interaction would turn toxic. Because we challenged ideas and concepts, as opposed to individuals or character, no one felt judged. Anger never reached toxic levels and none of our egos got in the way of working through issues. We prevented the toxins from entering our interactions. The result was that we uncovered problems in our work and developed solutions faster. Our open and honest feedback helped us grow as individuals, advance our careers, and improve our productivity as a team for the benefit of our company and clients. I'm proud to say that by the time we sold our company, the ePrize legal team had cleared more than 13,000 promotions in forty-four countries for many of the world's largest brands, with zero legal challenges. As a business unit, we achieved these results while operating close to a 90 percent margin from a profit-and-loss perspective.

A similar mentality exists in the arena of scientific research, where scientists are specifically trained and encouraged to question everything. The cornerstone of science is the falsifiable hypothesis, meaning that researchers must attempt to actually prove themselves wrong before they can claim something is true. In fact, they attempt to prove one another wrong all the time. In the short film *Science in America*, astrophysicist

Neil deGrasse Tyson explains how the scientific process leverages conflict to get to the truth:

> "One of the great things about science is that it is an entire exercise in finding what is true. [I make] an hypothesis, I test it. I get a result. A rival of mine double checks it because they think I might be wrong. They perform an even better experiment than I did, and they find out, "Hey, this experiment matches. Oh my gosh, we're on to something here." And out of this, rises a new emergent truth. It does it better than anything else that we have come up with as human beings."[9]

Just like my legal team at ePrize, members of the scientific community are able to engage in conflict without anger, fear, judgment, or ego reaching toxic levels because the scientific process has trained them to keep their survival emotions in check while they are attacking one another's findings. Of course, scientists are also human so emotions can still reach toxic levels, but the scientific method is designed to combat that. When the determination of truth takes priority over everything else, the opportunities for miscommunication, hurt feelings, and fear of retaliation are limited. Scientists are constantly challenging ideas and vehemently disagreeing with one another, which is inherent to scientific discovery. Since the scientific method requires these debates, there is little risk someone will take a challenge personally and get angry about

---

9   "Science In America." YouTube, uploaded by StarTalk, April 19, 2017. https://youtu.be/8MqTOEospfo.

it. Attacking someone's research certainly involves judgment, but it is a healthy dose of judgment, not a toxic one. And when a scientist's conclusions are proven wrong, it may bruise an ego, but that usually drives the scientist to work harder to make a greater contribution—an example of healthy ego at work. This type of healthy conflict drives scientific discovery and advances our species.

Embracing conflict without getting overly emotional or judgmental isn't just good for lawyers and scientists; it can benefit all of us in all areas of life. Even if an idea isn't good, there's often still value in expressing it and engaging in a debate about it. Ideally, someone will disagree with the idea and challenge your thinking, leading to an improvement. Our organizations are better off when we continually challenge ideas and processes, regardless of individual rank or title. The more we challenge, the more comfortable the process becomes and the easier it gets.

However, if we fail to keep these toxins in check, situations can quickly run out of control. When this happens, we can be pulled into four different traps that are very difficult to get out of.

THE CONFLICT TRAPS

There are four common traps we can be pulled into when toxins build in a conflict. When you keep the toxins in check, it's relatively easy to steer clear of the four traps. If you find that you already are in one of these traps, it's a more difficult situation, but there are still strategies and tools you can use to pull yourself out.

The Bully Trap

This is when bully-like behavior unintentionally creates toxic conflict. Often, the Bully Trap occurs when a toxic build-up of emotion causes one person's behavior to trigger a fight-or-flight response in someone else. For instance, if a leader loses their temper and yells at someone over a mistake, it may cause the other person to shut down and withdraw from a dialogue when they both need to communicate openly in order to fix the problem.

The Need-to-Win Trap

This is a scenario in which the competitive spirit gets out of hand, and the need to win a conflict gets in the way of a more important goal. We fall into the trap when we prioritize a short-term victory ahead of the primary objective that motivated us to enter a conflict in the first place. The need to win pulls us off track. For instance, you might find yourself needing to win a debate with an egotistical, rude coworker about a project, which is delaying your larger goal of getting buy-in from the rest of the team to move forward.

The Avoidance Trap

We fall into this trap when we avoid a conflict out of fear. In the context of the fight-or-flight response, this is *flight*. When fear reaches toxic levels, it prevents us from asking questions, admitting mistakes, offering ideas, or calling out problems. Toxic fear causes us to run from conflict rather than embrace it to make things better. For instance, the engineers at GM who knew about the ignition switch defect but didn't say anything were falling into the Avoidance Trap. By avoiding the issue, they ended up making the situation much worse in the long run.

The Judgment Trap

When our judgments of others mix with toxins like fear or anger, the resulting cocktail is a form of toxic judgment that can consume our energy and stop us from working successfully together. This is the Judgment Trap. We might allow judgments of someone else's life choices to prevent us from collaborating with them on a mutually beneficial project. Or we may waste time harboring angry judgments against someone who hurt us, instead of focusing on our personal and professional growth.

The rest of the book will break down each of the four Conflict Traps, showing you how they work and offering tools to help you pull out or to steer clear of them entirely. One of the big keys to making conflict work *for* you rather than *against* you is to keep emotions from reaching toxic levels. The tools in this book will help you not only keep your own emotions in check, but also to manage the emotions of others. This allows you to engage in necessary conflict while staying out of the Traps. As we dig deeper, you'll gain a new appreciation for how Vulcan Solutions' culture prevents toxins from building up, avoiding the Conflict Traps. You'll understand more clearly how the scientific method reduces toxic conflict in a different way. And you'll see exactly why we enjoyed such astounding success on the legal team at ePrize. The details may change, but the four Conflict Traps remain the same, and the tools to detox conflict never lose their effectiveness.

Professional mediators often use a tactic called shuttle diplomacy, which is extremely effective in preventing toxic emotions from creeping in and derailing a conflict. The mediator separates the parties into different rooms and shuttles back and forth to tell each person what the other said. Except the mediator doesn't repeat every word. Rather, the mediator removes the emotions and delivers only the facts. For instance, one party might say, "You tell that sonofabitch there's no way in hell I'm signing that!" The mediator might relay that comment to the other party as, "She appreciated the offer but isn't ready to accept it yet."

The mediator acts as a filter, removing toxic emotions from the dialogue and allowing the conflict to proceed in a calm and detached way. In the example above, the mediator filtered out anger from the communication. In other scenarios, a party's fear that an important issue won't be addressed is eliminated when the mediator demonstrates that he understands the issue and commits to communicating it properly. When one party judges another harshly, the mediator simply filters the judgment from their messages. The mediator can use the same technique to keep the parties' egos from getting in the way. Since every message is passed through the mediator, toxins that could pull people into destructive dialogue are cleansed.

Of course, shuttle diplomacy isn't practical for everyday use because most of us don't go through life with a mediator on hand who can filter messages between us and others. Instead, we need to engage conflict in real time, often without preparation or warning. The good news is that there are tactics we can employ to achieve the same benefits of shuttle diplomacy without having a professional mediator on hand. I will reveal those strategies in the chapters that follow.

First, we'll cover the Bully Trap, which Uma Thurman encountered unexpectedly when she was on set to shoot a scene for the movie *Kill Bill: Volume 2* with legendary Hollywood director Quentin Tarantino....

Embrace conflict
Healthy conflict propels people and organizations forward. Toxic conflict slows us down and causes pain.

Understand the roots
All conflict follows a set of simple, predictable patterns. There are two main reasons why engaging in healthy conflict is difficult for most people: the way our brains are wired, and the way we are raised.

- **Nature:** Our survival instincts have been bred over billions of years and are hard coded into our DNA. We have a natural fight-or-flight system that is automatically activated in response to conflict.
- **Nurture:** We are socialized from a young age with conflicting messages on how to manage conflict. We are taught to judge others while simultaneously viewing judgment as impolite; be open and honest with others, but to stay quiet if we don't have something nice to say. These conflicting messages are confusing.

The Conflict Toxins
Our nature and nurture produce four factors which are useful and productive when they stay in optimal ranges, but which become toxic when they fall below or rise above those optimal ranges. They are responsible for most unhealthy conflict.

- Fear
- Anger
- Judgment
- Ego

The Conflict Traps

There are four common traps we can be pulled into when toxins build in a conflict:

- Bully Trap
- Need-to-Win Trap
- Trap
- Judgment Trap

CHAPTER 2

The Bully Trap

In a shot that appears toward the end of *Kill Bill: Volume 2*, Uma Thurman's character speeds down a dirt road in a Karmann Ghia convertible on her way to actually kill Bill. For this shot, the camera was mounted on the rear of the car and the audience sees the back of Uma Thurman's head as her hair blows in the wind. Little does the casual viewer know that there is a tragic story behind this shot.

Quentin Tarantino is an award-winning writer and director; Uma Thurman is an A-list actor; and both are among the very best in the world at their crafts. They were arguably at the top of their game when they collaborated on this project, building off the success of *Pulp Fiction*. Their working relationship was producing great cinema, but even the best in the world aren't immune to toxic conflict. They were on location in Mexico filming the final scenes of *Kill Bill* (after nine months of shooting) when they were suddenly pulled headlong into the first Conflict Trap.

Uma later described Quentin as *"furious"* when he came to her trailer. The shoot was behind schedule and precious hours of sunlight were ticking away. Quentin was straining to complete principal photography for the three-and-a-half-hour epic. Budget constraints from Miramax had already forced the director to cut some of his favorite scenes. He needed one more shot at this location and he couldn't come back the following day. So when he heard Uma wasn't comfortable driving and wanted a stunt driver, the pressure ratcheted up. It was too late to hire a driver and Quentin knew getting Uma behind the wheel was his only chance at staying on schedule. The weight of the entire project was bearing down on him as he headed toward her trailer with a singular goal: get her to drive the car.

Uma was afraid of driving the car, and rightfully so. A crew member had told her the car wasn't safe. It had been converted from a stick shift to an automatic and the seat wasn't screwed down properly. This was a "Hollywood" car, not meant to be driven on real streets, and the road for this scene wasn't paved—it was sandy. Uma is an actor, not a trained stunt driver, and she thought the scene should be handled by a professional.

She tried to explain her fears about the car to Quentin, but he wasn't going to take "no" for an answer. He assured her the car was safe and said all she had to do was drive down a straight stretch of road. His instructions were: "Hit forty miles per hour or your hair won't blow the right way, and I'll make you do it again."

Against her better judgment, Uma caved to the pressure and agreed to do the shot. She climbed into the car she would refer to years later as a "deathbox."

"Action!" Tarantino called and Uma punched the gas, pointing the car along the sandy, unpaved road. Out of the corner of her eye she watched the speed, determined to hit forty mph so she would only have to film the harrowing scene once. As it turned out, the road was not straight. There was a hidden S-curve. The road had much more sand than expected and the car tires could not grip the surface to get the level of traction that most drivers—like Uma—are accustomed to. The raw footage from that day is frightening to watch and shows Uma desperately wrestling with the steering wheel as the car drifts off the road and crashes into a palm tree.

Uma Thurman suffered a concussion and permanent injuries to her neck and knees. Talk about toxic conflict. She recalls,

The steering wheel was at my belly, and my legs were jammed under me. I felt this searing pain and thought, 'Oh my God, I'm never going to walk again.' When I came back from the hospital in a neck brace with my knees damaged and a large massive egg on my head and a concussion, I wanted to see the car and I was very upset. Quentin and I had an enormous fight, and I accused him of trying to kill me. And he was very angry at that, I guess understandably, because he didn't feel he had tried to kill me.[10]

---

10 Dowd, Maureen. "This is Why Uma Thurman Is Angry." *New York Times*, February 13, 2018. https://www.nytimes.com/2018/02/03/opinion/sunday/this-is-why-uma-thurman-is-angry.html?. Accessed October 18, 2021.

Their close, collaborative relationship was forever damaged. The trust between them was broken, and their toxic conflict extended years beyond the day of the incident. Quentin Tarantino has cited it as one of his biggest regrets in life. He reflected many years later, "I talked her into getting in the car; I assured her the road was safe. And it wasn't."[11]

Up to that point, they had had a fantastic working relationship. Yet in the span of just a few minutes, they crossed a line they would never be able to retreat behind again. What caused their conflict to turn toxic? Quentin is not a bad person, nor is he mean-spirited. He is an excellent director; he's passionate about his craft and he has the forceful type of personality needed to get things done in Hollywood. But it was that same personality trait at play in this conflict. On that day in Mexico, he wasn't trying to act like a bully but his fear and anger reached toxic levels, pulling Quentin and Uma into the first conflict trap: the Bully Trap.

During adrenaline-fueled moments, we are all prone to falling into the Bully Trap. Quentin and Uma's conflict was a difficult situation, but there were other options: they could have consulted the crew member who said the car wasn't safe, or Quentin could have test-driven the route first. Had they properly assessed the danger of the situation, they certainly would have arranged for another driver, regardless of the cost. But none of those options were explored because they fell into the Bully Trap. So what is the Bully Trap, and what causes it?

---

11 Flemming, Mike. "Quentin Tarantino Explains Everything: Uma Thurman, The 'Kill Bill' Crash & Harvey Weinstein." Deadline.com, February 5, 2018. https://deadline.com/2018/02/quentin-tarantino-uma-thurman-harvey-weinstein-kill-bill-car-crash-new-york-times-1202278988/. Accessed October 18, 2021.

ACTING LIKE A BULLY

Some people are raised to behave like bullies. Others might pursue a goal so passionately they're willing to push through anything—or anyone—that gets in their way. Still others might feel angry about something and lack either the time or the ability to process that anger before giving feedback. There are lots of factors that give rise to bullying behavior, but not all bullying necessarily leads to the Bully Trap.

The Bully Trap refers only to situations in which someone bullies another person without intending to. Toxic emotions drive this behavior. It's hard to admit, but sometimes we may be seen as a bully in someone else's eyes. Most of us have fallen into the Bully Trap at one time or another, and when bullying behavior starts, it acts like fertilizer for toxic conflict.

The Bully Trap doesn't refer to the traditional scenario of a bully on the playground who takes another kid's lunch money. Rather, the Bully Trap occurs when a toxic buildup of emotion evokes behavior that triggers a fight or flight response in someone else—like when Quentin Tarantino's behavior triggered a flight response in Uma Thurman, which caused her to withdraw from the conversation. Other examples include an employee whose boss belittles him in front of his peers, so he quits and badmouths his former company to everyone he meets; or a student whose self-esteem and long-term academic performance is damaged after a teacher berates her for missing an assignment.

The Bully Trap occurs in high-stress scenarios when our emotions are raw and the pressure is on. These are optimal conditions for feelings of anger, fear, and ego to elevate to toxic levels. For example, a manager might feel angry about having an underperforming team, which reflects poorly on him. Not only does his ego take a hit, he might be stressed about getting chewed out by his own boss, and fearful of how the team's performance will impact his career. These toxic emotions could drive the manager straight into the Bully Trap. Without intending to behave like a bully, he might take his frustration out on his direct reports through belittling, threatening, or scolding. This behavior is a hallmark of bad leadership, but sadly it is commonplace in the business world.

WHY BULLYING DOESN'T WORK

What's wrong with a little bullying if it ultimately helps get the job done? We can't go around avoiding conflict. After all, standing up to others is courageous, right?

Bullying is an incredibly ineffective method for handling disagreements and dealing with conflict. Sure, a boss who berates his employees might drive them to work harder in the short term, out of fear. But as Dacher Keltner, a professor of psychology at University of California, Berkeley, has observed in his research, this kind of abuse ultimately tarnishes the reputations of executives and undermines their ability to lead.[12] It also creates stress and anxiety among colleagues; diminishes resilience and creativity in the group; and drags down team member engagement and performance. In a poll of 800 managers and employees across seventeen indus-

---

12 Keltner, Dacher. "Don't Let Power Corrupt You." *Harvard Business Review* (October 2016). https://hbr.org/2016/10/dont-let-power-corrupt-you. Accessed October 18, 2021.

tries, about half the respondents who reported being treated rudely at work said they deliberately decreased their effort or lowered the quality of their work in response.[13] Operating in an abusive work environment is distracting, lowers quality, engenders ill will, and destroys loyalty.

The main drivers of the Bully Trap are toxic levels of emotion, predominantly anger. If we speak to someone while we're angry or frustrated, those emotions will come through in our communication. When toxic emotions interfere with our ability to communicate, the conflict worsens. The other person feels attacked and their defense mechanisms kick in. This perceived attack can trigger our survival instincts and overpower our rational decision making. This is helpful when facing down a cougar in the wild, but destructive when resolving delicate issues with friends, family, or coworkers. Outside of immediate physical threats, we must cleanse the toxic emotions from our conflicts.

When leaders have the habit of falling into the Bully Trap, we tend to avoid them. We adopt a "flight" response to those who bring toxic emotions into conflicts because we don't feel comfortable pointing out mistakes or asking for help. Consequently, we also avoid engaging in the healthy conflicts that drive progress. If left unchecked, this pattern leads to a culture of silence and avoidance, resulting in problems going unaddressed—such as the ignition switch defect at General Motors.

We don't always avoid bullies; sometimes we fight back. Employees may not openly challenge a bullying boss for fear

---

13 Ibid.

of being fired, but they may resort to more subversive tactics like manipulation or gossip. This "fight" response also leads team members to bully each other. They channel negativity toward their teammates and resort to finger-pointing. This, in turn, releases even more toxins into the work environment and breeds a culture rife with toxic conflict. A leader's bullying behavior motivates employees to devote time and energy to undermining the leader and blaming coworkers; time and energy that is no longer devoted to serving client interests or improving the business.

GIVING FEEDBACK

The Bully Trap also does tremendous damage when leaders attempt to give feedback to team members. When toxic levels of anger trigger a fight-or-flight response, the amygdala shuts down a person's ability to intellectually process feedback. This prevents us from seeing the solution, or from even understanding the bully's perspective. A bully can huff and puff until blue in the face, but it doesn't help resolve the conflict because the listener literally cannot hear what's being said.

People don't want to feel bad, so when giving feedback turns into bullying, their defense mechanisms kick in. They engage in denial and dismiss the feedback or the person giving it: *I didn't do anything wrong. My boss must be having a bad day and is taking it out on me.* Or they might engage in projection, blaming their behavior on someone else's flaw: *This isn't my fault. I was simply trying to cover up Bob's mistake.* Whatever they're doing, they're not listening to the feedback. Their defense mechanisms are hard at work protecting them from the attack.

Giving direct feedback is a critical part of every leader's job and an essential part of a healthy relationship. While the example of a leader giving feedback to an employee is helpful to frame the issue, this goes far beyond the work context. The problem of the Bully Trap arises in virtually every relationship. The key to engaging in healthy conflict in these situations is to detox our feedback to ensure that we don't fall into the Bully Trap along the way. But why do so many of us fall into the trap in the first place?

When our anger, fear, and ego reach toxic levels, they can trigger the Bully Trap, and there are three factors that contribute to this toxicity: Authority, Passion, and Depersonalization.

1. Authority

The first factor that helps push anger, fear, and ego into toxic levels is authority. They say absolute power corrupts absolutely, and studies show they are right. Even compassionate people can fall into the Bully Trap when they reach a position of authority.

In companies that go through rapid growth, strong individual performers are promoted outside their skillset into positions of leadership. It's a little silly when you think about it: *"You're doing such a good job in your current role that we're promoting you into a leadership position for which you have no training and no experience, and in which you haven't demonstrated any proficiency."* No one actually says this, but it happens all the time. Hard working, high-performing people suddenly find themselves in roles for which they're not qualified. Some realize they're ill-equipped to lead and their fear of failure spikes to toxic levels, which then pushes them to overcompensate for their lack of ability with aggression. Others lack awareness of their underqualification because when they are promoted, their egos rise to toxic levels that prevent them from acknowledging their shortcomings. They won't seek to develop or improve their leadership skills.

Not knowing how to lead, many resort to one of the least common denominators: displays of power. Research indicates we are more susceptible to the pull of the Bully Trap when we have power over someone else. An example of how quickly power can pull people into the Bully Trap comes from the famous 1971 Stanford Prison Experiment.[14] Initially planned for two weeks, the study had to be abandoned after only six days.

In this study, volunteer students were randomly assigned to act as either a "prisoner" or a "guard" in a simulated prison. It didn't take long for the guards to abuse their power. They forced inmates to clean toilets by hand, perform jumping jacks for hours, sleep without beds, and live without waste buckets in their rooms. The abuse was so bad that some of the "prisoners" broke down in hysterical crying fits. The only difference between the guards and prisoners had been a coin toss, but as soon as some of the students were given power, their ego and anger elevated to toxic levels and they slid right into the Bully Trap.

Authority tends to shift people toward a more egocentric perspective, making them less considerate of others. A 2006 study from Northwestern University investigated the

---

14 The Stanford Prison Experiment website. https://www.prisonexp. org/. Accessed October 18, 2021.

impact feelings of power had on an individual's perspective.[15] Participants were asked to draw a capital 'E' on their forehead with a washable marker. Those instructed to think of a time when they had power over another person preferred to orient the 'E' towards themselves (not easily readable to viewers). The participants who didn't think about feeling powerful preferred to write the 'E' backwards so it could be read by others. The experiment suggests that power makes people more egocentric and less considerate of others. When some people are placed in positions of authority with significant responsibility, there is a tendency to think of those under their authority as assets to achieve certain goals. When they encounter difficulty in reaching those goals, egocentric leaders are more likely to allow their frustration to turn toxic, which is usually expressed as bullying.

Power can also be derived from wealth or credentials. Studies show wealth and credentials can elevate ego to toxic levels that promote bullying behavior. UC Irvine researcher Paul Piff and his colleague Dachler Keltner found that, while drivers of less expensive vehicles (Dodge Colts, Plymouth Satellites, etc.) always ceded the right-of-way to pedestrians at a crosswalk, people driving luxury cars such as BMWs and Mercedes yielded only 54 percent of the time.[16]

---

15 Galinsky, A.D. et al. "Power and Perspectives Not Taken." First published in December 2006 issue of *Psychological Science*. http://homepages.se.edu/cvonbergen/files/2012/12/Power-and-Perspectives-Not-Taken1.pdf.

16 Keltner, Dacher. "Don't Let Power Corrupt You." *Harvard Business Review* (October 2016), https://hbr.org/2016/10/dont-let-power-corrupt-you. Accessed October 18, 2021.

In a business context, studies show that people in positions of corporate power are three times as likely as those at the lower rungs of the ladder to interrupt coworkers, multitask during meetings, raise their voices, and say insulting things at the office.[17] Most of us don't know what power will do to us until we experience it, but these experiments demonstrate the natural draw for normal people to fall into the Bully Trap when put in an authoritative position without adequate training.

2. Passion

The second way we can experience toxic anger and fall into the Bully Trap is when we are emotionally invested in an outcome. This was one of the factors that led Quentin Tarantino to bully Uma Thurman into driving the car. He had a detailed vision of exactly what he wanted, right down to the precise speed she needed to drive so that her hair would blow a certain way. His passion for these details and his ability to make them a reality are two character traits that make him a renowned filmmaker. On this occasion, he was in execution mode and working against tight budget constraints; he was going to get the shot before sundown. Nothing was going to stop him.

Passion impaired Quentin's decision-making. His fear of missing this shot was elevated to a toxic level, and he fell into the Bully Trap. It's interesting to note how Uma's and Quentin's memories of the situation differ. Years later, when speaking to *New York Times* reporter Maureen Dowd, Uma

---

17   Ibid.

described Quentin as being "furious" when he came to her trailer to tell her to drive the car.[18] However, in an interview with Deadline, Quentin recalls:

"I'm sure when it was brought up to me, that I rolled my eyes and was irritated. But I'm sure I wasn't in a rage and I wasn't livid. I didn't go barging into Uma's trailer, screaming at her to get into the car. I can imagine maybe rolling my eyes..."[19]

Memories can be a funny thing, and our individual perceptions are influenced by our emotional state. It is impossible to know exactly what happened in Uma's trailer, but we do know that she felt bullied, while he felt he did not bully her. We also know that they are both reasonable people. As I mentioned earlier, though, sometimes we can be seen as a bully in someone else's eyes. We don't *feel* like a bully, and we certainly don't *intend* to bully the other person, but passion can place reasonable people on the delivery side of the Bully Trap.

Obviously, Quentin Tarantino didn't intend to put Uma Thurman in harm's way, and he never would have let her get behind the wheel of that car if he thought there was a chance she could get hurt. But his passion filtered out information

---

18   Dowd, Maureen. "This is Why Uma Thurman Is Angry." *New York Times*, February 13, 2018. https://www.nytimes.com/2018/02/03/opinion/sunday/this-is-why-uma-thurman-is-angry.html?. Accessed October 18, 2021.

19   Flemming, Mike. "Quentin Tarantino Explains Everything: Uma Thurman, The 'Kill Bill' Crash & Harvey Weinstein." Deadline.com, February 5, 2018. https://deadline.com/2018/02/quentin-tarantino-uma-thurman-harvey-weinstein-kill-bill-car-crash-new-york-times-1202278988/. Accessed October 18, 2021.

that suggested he ought to delay the shot. The combination of passion, authority, and anger created a toxic cocktail that pulled him into the Bully Trap.

3. Depersonalization

The third type of situation in which we are more likely to allow our emotions to reach toxic levels is when we fail to see others as fully human. In the Stanford Prison Experiment, prisoners were forced to refer to themselves by numbers rather than names. This is a well-known method of depersonalization. Looking at the most extreme examples, researchers who study genocide have theorized that depersonalization is a major factor that influences ordinary people to commit mass killings. During the Holocaust, Nazi propagandists knew that when people view members of a specific ethnic group as being less human, or more like animals, it makes it easier to ignore their humanity and treat them cruelly.

To a much lesser degree, the same effect can play out in daily life. I once saw a parking enforcement officer put a ticket on someone's windshield as the driver was walking toward his car. The driver yelled, "Thanks a lot, you bastard! I'll bet that made your day." The driver didn't see the officer as a fully formed human, but instead saw him as a one-dimensional "meter maid." The driver spoke to him as if the officer lived his entire life wearing that parking enforcement uniform, lived in a parking-enforcement themed house, and sat around with other parking enforcement officers sharing stories of putting tickets on cars in their free time. This depersonalized viewpoint allowed the driver's anger to grow to toxic levels, whereas a more humanized view of the officer likely would have kept that emotion in check.

When we define others by the limited roles they play in our lives, we're more susceptible to the pulls of the Bully Trap. All day long, we interact with people in depersonalized ways, and there is no shortage of situations where we will be influenced to act like a bully, especially when we are stressed. Take road rage, for example.

On the road, we typically define others based solely on how they drive, rather than by who they are as individuals. Most of us have been cut off by someone on the freeway. I admit that I have felt flashes of toxic anger toward other drivers. *That asshole just cut me off; he probably beats his children. I hope she crashes her car. That is a horrible human being. She can't possibly have any friends.*

Comedian Louis C.K. does a bit on how driving brings out the worst in him.[20] He says that when he's behind the wheel of his car, he has a different set of values. He is the worst person he can be. Someone once drifted into his lane for a second and he yelled, "Hey, fuck you! Worthless piece of shit!" Outside of a car, though, is that even remotely okay? If you were in an elevator and someone leaned into your personal space for half a second, would you turn to them and say, "Hey, fuck you! Worthless piece of shit!" Of course not. No one would ever do that. But put a couple pieces of glass and some road between you and another driver, Louis says, and there's suddenly nothing you wouldn't say.

---

20 Louis C.K.: On driving – HBO *Oh My God* Comedy Special.

When someone is depersonalized, it is easier for our anger to rise to toxic levels, and most of us are capable of behavior we would never consider if we had a human connection with that person. This is one of the reasons why we see so much anger and cruelty on social media. The detachment and anonymity of social media makes it easier for people to let toxic anger pull them into the Bully Trap. They feel emboldened to type hateful things from their living room couch that they would never say to someone face-to-face. Chatting with a "user" online feels very different from talking to a human being (who didn't just put a parking ticket on your car).

While depersonalization likely was not a factor between Quentin and Uma on the set of *Kill Bill*, some directors might view actors and crew members merely based on their roles, not bothering to learn their names or anything about them. That's depersonalizing.

AVOIDING THE BULLY TRAP

There are some techniques that cleanse toxins from our confrontations so we can communicate effectively and avoid falling into the Bully Trap. Whether we're giving feedback to a coworker, loved one, business partner, or friend, the same dynamics are always present. Use the following tips to detox your emotions and engage in healthy conflict.

Shopping List Voice

One of the best tools for confronting an issue with someone is the Shopping List Voice. When I gave my very first speech about how to handle conflict to a group of CEOs, this was one of the two techniques that I received an outpouring of positive feedback on (the other was Don't Get Mad at Penguins, which you'll see later). When you use the Shopping List Voice, others will be able to receive your message without having their defense mechanisms triggered.

Finding your Shopping List Voice is simple. Imagine your roommate, spouse, or parent is heading to the grocery store and asks whether you need anything. You want to make a cake and need a number of ingredients. Think about the tone of voice you would use to convey the list of items. You would speak calmly, dispassionately, and without anger: *"It'd be great if you can pick up some eggs, flour, milk, sugar, frosting, and sprinkles."* It's the same tone you might use to give someone directions to your house. You get the idea.

Now imagine you are a leader at a company when a major client calls to terminate their contract. They explain that one of your team members, Bill, made some costly mistakes. You're understandably angry with Bill when you get off the phone. Obviously, you need to address the issue with him. The question is whether or not you will allow your anger to rise to toxic levels in your communication. Consider these two possible ways of delivering the message:

Option 1: You slam down the phone, march over to Bill's desk, and yell at him. "HEY! I JUST GOT OFF THE PHONE WITH THE CLIENT! THEY SAID YOU SENT DELIVERABLES WITH A TON OF ERRORS! THEY HAD TO REDO YOUR WORK AND MISSED A DEADLINE AS A RESULT! AND THEY SAID THIS ISN'T THE FIRST TIME YOU'VE DONE THAT! SO GUESS WHAT!

THEY FIRED US! THAT'S RIGHT, THAT WAS A $2M ACCOUNT THAT IS NO LONGER A CLIENT OF THIS FIRM BECAUSE YOU CAN'T FIGURE OUT HOW TO DO YOUR JOB! GET YOUR SHIT TOGETHER, OR I'LL FIND SOMEONE WHO KNOWS HOW TO NOT LOSE MULTI-MILLION DOLLAR CLIENTS!"

A rant at this volume all but guarantees you've fallen into the Bully Trap. Approximately three seconds into that rant, Bill stopped listening. Either his defense mechanisms kicked in and he started focusing instead on why this wasn't his fault, or his amygdala shut down the neural pathways to the thinking portion of his brain, and he literally could not process the message.

Option 2: You communicate the same message but in a Shopping List Voice—a dispassionate, matter-of-fact tone. "I just got off the phone with the client. They said you sent deliverables with many errors, and they had to redo your work. They missed a deadline as a result. They also said this isn't the first time this has happened, and they have terminated our agreement as a result. That's a $2M account that is no longer a client of this firm."

The substance of the message in both scenarios is identical. With Option 1, we lost Bill within the first three seconds, either because brain chemistry shut down his ability to process information, or because his defense mechanisms were hard at work protecting him from the attack. However, with Option 2, Bill probably did not like what he heard but at least he was able to listen to and process the message.

Adopting the right tone is enough to avoid the Bully Trap in even the most challenging conversations. When you consciously adopt a Shopping List Voice, you'll find it easier to focus on delivering the message so the other person receives it well.

The Shopping List Voice cleanses toxic anger from confrontational situations. When you communicate without anger, there's nothing to trigger the other person's defense mechanisms. They will remain receptive to your feedback and focused on understanding the message, instead of rationalizing why they should ignore it or blame someone else. They may not like what you are saying, but they will hear it. And if you let them know the feedback is primarily for their benefit, they are more likely to be grateful for it: "Bill, I want you to see how these types of mistakes can impact client relationships so that you can be successful here and avoid situations like this in the future."

On the set of *Kill Bill*, things might have turned out differently if Tarantino had followed this principle. Had he stopped for a few moments on the way to Uma's trailer to dial things down and focus on a Shopping List Voice, he might have spoken to her in a way that wouldn't have caused her to shut down; they could have engaged in a dialogue that explored other options.

As a bonus tip, whenever you have to give harsh feedback, take the opportunity to reaffirm the person:

"Bill, this is a horrible mistake, but you're not horrible. You're a smart, very capable person with a great future ahead of you. My hope is that you will use this incident as a growth opportunity. Six months from now, people will look back and say, 'Wow, he really screwed up, but ever since then he's been a rock star: high quality deliverables, on time, and with a great attitude. I look forward to working with him again.'

Framing the mistake as an opportunity for growth changes the dynamic. When we communicate from a place of support, we neutralize toxic emotions and avoid the Bully Trap.

Check Yourself Before You Wreck Yourself

Since power and authority both unconsciously promote bullying behavior, self-awareness can act as an antidote. When you interact with someone over whom you have authority, take note of the feelings that accompany your power. Those feelings can reach toxic levels and cause us to engage in rash and rude behavior. When we observe and label these feelings, we can detox their impact. This keeps our behavior in check. When we feel frustrated (perhaps because someone on our team made a costly mistake) and we take a moment to note our anger, we are less likely to bully someone.

Carving out time for mindfulness and self-reflection on a regular basis will increase self-awareness. This can be as simple as taking a few minutes each day to sit comfortably and focus on your breathing, but there are many mindfulness techniques at your fingertips. A quick internet search will point you to instructional videos, articles, and books. (And the benefits of daily mindfulness go far beyond detoxing conflict, so check it out.)

A little bit of humility goes a long way to keep power-induced behavior in check, and you can cultivate it by focusing on gratitude and generosity. If you have achieved a position of authority through hard work, *great!* You probably deserve it. But you should also be grateful for the opportunities that got you there and the people you worked with along the way. Express gratitude on a regular basis and be generous. Thank people often, send emails of appreciation, and publicly acknowledge the contributions of others. Not only will these small gestures improve performance and culture, they will keep the toxic effects of power and authority at bay.

No Venting

Setbacks can happen without warning, and the toxins can come flooding into our interactions regardless of any methods we practice on a regular basis. Sometimes people on our teams make costly mistakes, and our natural human response is to get angry. However, a display of anger when giving corrective feedback is not a demonstration of strength. It is a demonstration of weakness—an inability to control our emotions. The question is whether we're going to control our anger or allow it to control us. The answer determines whether we demonstrate good leadership or bad, and whether or not we fall into the Bully Trap.

Here's a bright-line rule for giving feedback: no venting. While unleashing an emotional tirade on someone might be a healthy, cathartic exercise for you, it's not mutually beneficial. You'll have released the anger, but you only dumped it on the other person. There might even be some cosmic justice in that; it's only fair that the person who caused the problem suffers the consequences of your anger. But that's not feedback. That's just you beating up on someone. If we're angry, we need to process our anger before giving feedback so we don't come from an emotional place. We must cleanse those toxic emotions from our communication.

You might be furious that someone on your team messed up on a big order for a new client. But storming over to the person to give him a "piece of your mind" is a recipe for getting caught in the Bully Trap. Passion and authority can both lead to the Bully Trap, so there are two forces working against you. The urge to give immediate feedback will be strong. Resist it. If the situation can wait, it's best to sleep on it. Let the anger dissipate. If it's a more pressing matter, find ways to cool off.

If you have the ability to work out, go for a run, journal, or meditate, great. Punch a pillow or take a quick walk. I'm sure you've been angry and calmed yourself down before, so do whatever has worked in the past. At an absolute minimum, take a few minutes to breathe slowly, deeply, and deliberately, if that's all you have time for. Do what you can to set aside your emotions and dial down the passion.

A good way of gauging whether you have defused enough anger to neutralize its toxic effect on your communication is to practice the Shopping List Voice before giving someone feedback. If you cannot maintain a Shopping List Voice during your rehearsal, you aren't ready. Time to squeeze a stress ball, count backwards from ten, or do whatever it takes to let off some steam. Once you can deliver the entire message in your Shopping List Voice, you're ready to share your feedback.

Clarify

Anger clouds our ability to communicate clearly. In fact, anger causes us to communicate before we even have a clear idea of the specific message we want to get across. Put another way, anger makes us act without thinking.

If your goal is to give feedback, you must clarify in your own mind the goal of the feedback you're about to give. *This person needs to understand the consequences of her behavior so she can take corrective action and avoid problems like this moving forward.* This will help cleanse toxic anger, and it will tighten up your message. If your anger is still hot, try another quick breathing exercise to calm down, and then try to clarify your goal again. Maybe you want the other person to improve. Maybe you want them to be more considerate. Whatever your goal is, getting clarity around it will help.

Humanize the Other Person

To combat depersonalization, a great tactic is to humanize the other person. Before sitting down to confront someone about their behavior, spend a few minutes thinking about what you have in common. What are your shared interests, objectives, and backgrounds? Also think about what their typical day is like. Do they live with others? Are they engaged or married? Do they drop the kids off at school on the way to work every morning? This simple exercise broadens your perspective and helps you see the other person as a complete human, rather than a one-dimensional character who made a mistake.

If you're speaking with someone face-to-face, make an effort to notice five to ten small details about them before you start talking. This has the added benefit of giving you something active to do while getting you out of your own head at the top of the conversation.

One of the most important questions you can ask yourself before a difficult conversation is, "What does this person want?" Then ask, "When have I wanted the same thing?"

For the most part, we all want the same things in life. We want to feel safe, loved, important, cared for, and proud. We want to succeed, connect, and stay healthy. Take a second to look at conflict through the eyes of the other person. Ask yourself what they want and when you have wanted the same thing. Empathize with your shared humanity before you start talking.

If you're speaking by phone, pull up a photo of the other person. Try to generate a sense of connection before you dial. What can you learn about the person in sixty seconds? A wealth of information is available with just a few clicks.

Imagine if Quentin Tarantino had done this on the way to Uma Thurman's trailer: *What Uma really wants is to feel safe. I can relate to that.* We've all gone through experiences that made us wish for safety. It would have taken only a few moments for Quentin to reflect on this, build some empathy, and reduce his toxic anger before their conversation. During their exchange, her need to feel safe would have carried the same weight as his need to get the shot, instead of his need overpowering hers.

Responding to a Bully

So far, we have covered how to avoid falling into the Bully Trap when you are the bully. But what if the person we are dealing with comes at us with toxic emotions? This section will cover some actions we can take to effectively respond to bullying behavior.

Back on the set of *Kill Bill*, there were alternatives to Uma driving the car, but Quentin and Uma didn't explore those options because they were caught in the Bully Trap. Quentin's fear of going over budget coupled with the urgency of the moment led to toxic anger, which he directed toward Uma (fight response). Uma was fearful of driving an unsafe car, but when confronted with Quentin's furious attack, she caved to the pressure (flight response).

When we are bullied, it's natural for us to feel toxic anger in response. This triggers a fight reaction, which can escalate the conflict. Alternatively, we might experience toxic fear that causes us to withdraw and shut down so we can weather the storm. Most of the time, however, we can defuse these situations by dispassionately making people aware of our concerns. This is a great use of the Shopping List Voice: *I know you want the shot done a certain way, but I don't feel safe. A crew member told me the car is dangerous. Can we at least consider another option?*

A dispassionate response helps to prevent our toxic emotions from escalating the conflict. It can defuse the other person's anger, reducing it to a non-toxic level and steering the conflict out of the Bully Trap. Responding to anger with a calm, steady tone is not easy. It is a learned skill that, with practice, you can master.

When you can see the Bully Trap coming and steer clear of it, you are disrupting your instinctive responses and defusing toxic conflict. The next time you're confronted with bullying behavior, think to yourself, *Oh, this is the Bully Trap I read about.* That recognition takes less than one second, which is all you need to stop your instinctive response. At that point, you're free to choose how you respond instead of your amygdala triggering an automatic fight-or-flight reaction.

Once we develop this presence of mind, we can make calculated inferences about the person bullying us. Maybe this is a generally good person who doesn't intend to cause us harm. Maybe the bully is just venting. We can respond dispassionately and put the brakes on the Bully Trap before the conflict escalates:

> "I don't think your intent is to attack me but that's how your tone of voice is making me feel. I value your feedback, and if I've done something wrong, I need to be held accountable. I want to hear what you have to say so I can learn, but that's hard to do with this tone of conversation."

Be sure to say things like this using a Shopping List Voice. A dispassionate tone is critical. State the facts simply and convey the information without getting worked up. Keep the tone calm, clear, and precise. This is not easy at first, but I regularly hear from people how easy it becomes after a little practice.

WE ALWAYS HAVE A CHOICE

I recently gave a guest-lecture to a private equity class at the Ross School of Business, University of Michigan. Most of the students were preparing to graduate and begin careers at investment banks and private equity firms on Wall Street. These are highly coveted jobs with great pay and enviable perks, but these work environments are also notoriously abusive. Some of the students' questions focused on how to deal with bullying bosses. They'd heard stories and were scared (and justifiably so). Wall Street is not a flowery, comforting place. It is filled with type-A personalities, fierce competition, and harsh criticism.

After sharing some of the tactics covered above, I gave my best advice: have thick skin. It was unrealistic to think they could change the environment of Wall Street. If they were concerned about their ability to thrive in that culture, then they should seriously question whether it was the right career path.

Ultimately, we always have a choice. If you're not a shark, don't swim with sharks. If you don't like the sight of blood, don't be a surgeon. If you're afraid of heights, don't wash windows on skyscrapers. We can't always control our environment, but we do have a great deal of control over the positions we voluntarily put ourselves into. We also have control over how we react to stubborn people who refuse to change, which is the focus of Chapter 7: Don't Get Mad at Penguins Because They Can't Fly.

If someone continues to act like a bully toward you after you've tried these tools, it might be time to conclude that this person will not change. If they're not willing to treat you with respect after repeated attempts, accept that and stop fighting it. Then you can make an informed decision about how to respond next. The ultimate answer will depend on the circumstances. The point is that you can choose how to react based on an intellectual analysis, not an instinctive response.

These tools will help you manage the Bully Trap. We will later look at how they can be used with some of the other traps as well. However, a very different approach was needed when I was on the brink of making a terrible mistake in Judge Morcum's courtroom. I was caught deep in the second conflict trap—the Need-to-Win Trap....

UNDERSTANDING THE BULLY TRAP

Not all bullying is a trap

The Bully Trap refers to situations in which toxic anger, fear, or ego drive bullying behavior with the unintended consequence of making conflict worse, or creating toxic conflict where none existed.

The Bully Trap occurs in high-stress scenarios

When our emotions are raw and the pressure is on, these are optimal conditions for feelings of anger, fear, and ego to elevate to toxic levels. This drives behavior that can unintentionally trigger someone else's fight-or-flight response.

Three factors that feed toxins

These factors often lead to toxic anger, fear, and ego, pulling us into the Bully Trap.

- **Authority:** Even compassionate people can fall into the Bully Trap when in a position of authority. In positions of power, we adopt a more ego-centric perspective, making us less considerate and more likely to bully others.
- **Passion:** Sometimes we can be seen as a bully in someone else's eyes because we are passionate, and our excitement comes off as aggression.
- **Depersonalization:** When we view others solely based on the roles they play in our lives, we're susceptible to the Bully Trap.

The Bully Trap does significant damage

Bullying shuts down communication. In the workplace, this promotes undermining, manipulation, and more bullying. It takes energy away from positive growth. Bullying destroys otherwise productive feedback.

TOOLS TO OVERCOME THE BULLY TRAP

Shopping List Voice
Detox communication by speaking in a matter-of-fact, dispassionate tone, like you are telling your friend what you'd like them to pick up for you at the store.

No venting
Never use feedback to beat up on somebody (that is a sign of weakness, not strength). Process anger before giving feedback. Control your emotions; don't allow them to control you.

Reaffirm
When delivering harsh feedback, take the opportunity to reaffirm the person.

Clarify
Clarify the goal of message before you deliver it. This neutralizes toxins and tightens up communication.

Humanize the other person
Before confronting someone, spend a few minutes thinking about things you have in common.

Responding to a bully
All of the above are just as effective when on the receiving end of the Bully Trap.

CHAPTER 3

The Need-to-Win Trap

When I walked into Judge Morcum's courtroom, the only sound in the world was my heart pounding through my chest, sending adrenaline surging through my veins. All my senses were heightened and I was ready for battle. The moment I'd been working toward for years had finally arrived. This was my opportunity to prove myself, achieve justice, and serve my client. This was my shot to *win*. I didn't know it, but I was about to step into the second Conflict Trap: the Need-to-Win Trap.

That was twenty-five years ago, but I still remember every detail like it happened this morning. The case was simple: my client, Fiona, was a single mother of three who'd been driving one day when a bus suddenly swerved into her lane and banged her car, forcing her off the road and into a telephone pole. The bus didn't even stop. The accident left her partially disabled with a future full of surgeries and pain.

I took Fiona's case and worked like hell on it. I subpoenaed records, deposed witnesses, and even tracked down the exact bus that was driven on the day of the accident looking for traces of paint from Fiona's car. But that was a dead end (those buses have dings and scratches all over them). The bus company denied the accident happened and the driver testified he couldn't remember anything about that day. They hired one of the biggest law firms in town. They had more money, more lawyers, and more resources than we did. All we had was the word of my client. We were outgunned and it wasn't looking good. That's when I found a smoking gun.

Buried among the thousands of pages of documents the bus company threw at me was the log sheet for the bus on the day of the accident, written in the bus driver's own handwriting. If you've ever seen emotion translated into the written word, this was it. This guy was *mad*. He'd been called in unexpectedly to cover for a sick driver. Written in all caps at the top of the page—the pen almost tearing through the paper—were the words, **"THIS WAS MY OFF DAY!!!"** In the notes section he'd scrawled, **"This is an overloaded route with too many rowdy passengers!"**

Another note read: **"Per dispatch, pedal to metal back to station."** That last entry was made six minutes before the accident, and the log sheet confirmed the bus was in the exact location of the accident at the precise time my client had been run off the road. The jury would no longer have to take my client at her word. The bus company's own records proved the bus was at the time and place of the accident, filled with rowdy passengers, and being driven by a distracted, angry bus driver who had just been told to put the "pedal to the metal." Staring down at that log sheet, I was angry and offended by the company's deceit and refusal to accept responsibility for the accident. *How dare they think they could get away with this?*

For the first time since I took the case, I felt confident I was going to win.

My plan was to sit back and wait for the bus driver to deny the accident on the witness stand in front of the jury. Once I'd set the trap, I was going to spring the log sheet on him in a moment of courtroom glory most lawyers only dream of.

So, there I was in Judge Morcum's courtroom, ready to lay waste to my opponents. I didn't know it, but something that had happened more than thirty years earlier was about to dramatically impact the next thirty minutes of this case.

Back in 1964, Claudia House Morcum wasn't a judge. She was a young African American lawyer who went down to Mississippi with a group of other young lawyers to represent civil rights workers who were getting into trouble with local law enforcement. The workers were in Mississippi registering Black people to vote, and the local sheriffs didn't take too kindly to their efforts. Earlier that summer, local police had arrested three civil rights workers on a bogus speeding violation. The civil rights workers were never seen alive again.

It turns out that my father was one of those young lawyers with Claudia Morcum in Mississippi, and they shared a close bond forged under the pressure of those extreme circumstances.

Three decades later, in Judge Morcum's courtroom where I waited eagerly to lay waste to my opponents, I had no idea about her shared experience with my dad. But it might have been the reason she was about to save me from myself.

Like any good judge, she called the lawyers into her chambers to see if we could settle the case before picking a jury. When she spoke to me alone, she said I had a weak case, and I should accept the settlement offer from the bus company. I tipped my hand and showed her the log sheet, but I asked her not to tell the opposing counsel I had it. She looked it over and then called the other lawyer back into her chambers:

Judge Morcum: You need to increase your offer.

Defense attorney: Your honor, I don't believe the accident even happened.

Judge Morcum: Well *I* believe it happened, and I believe *he* will convince a jury that it happened.

Then she leaned on this lawyer like I've never seen a judge pressure a lawyer before. At one point, she picked up the phone and asked, "Do you need me to call your client to get more authority for you?" Ultimately, they increased their previous offer by more than ten times.

I sat back smugly and said, "I'll relay the offer to my client, as I'm required to do, but it's not enough." Judge Morcum asked the other lawyer to excuse us for a second time. Now it was my turn in the hot seat.

Judge Morcum: What the hell do you think you're doing?

Me: Judge, they hurt my client. They *lied* about it, they covered it up, and now they think they can get away with it by throwing her a few extra bucks?! No, I can win this case. I'm going to expose this injustice for what it is and expose them for who they are.

Judge Morcum: [slowly shaking her head] I do not need *you* to lecture *me* about injustice, young man. They just offered your client more money than she's ever dreamed of. Money that will change her life and the lives of her children. And you're going to gamble that by going to trial? Your job is to achieve the best result possible for your client. And I'm telling you, you've just done it.

I realized conflict had gotten the best of me. I was so focused on winning in court that I wasn't willing to consider a great settlement. I wouldn't accept anything less than absolute victory. Sure, I had the log sheet, but anything can happen during trial. Rejecting their settlement offer at that point would have been reckless, and my client could have ended up with nothing. I had allowed my ego and anger to build up to toxic levels, causing me to put my need to win before my client's needs. Luckily, Judge Morcom chose to save me (and my client) from myself.

One of the lessons from this story is that emotion can take conflict into unproductive, even destructive territory. We tend to rely on feelings of anger or self-righteousness to build ourselves up into feeling powerful. The irony is that these emotions can be our greatest weaknesses. Anger and ego can reach toxic levels and pull us into the Need-to-Win Trap. When we are caught in this trap, it's easy to lose sight of our true objective, blinded by our desire to beat the other party.

THE NEED TO WIN

The defining moment of this trap is when the desire to win a conflict eclipses a more important goal. When we prioritize a short-term victory over the primary objective that motivated us to enter a conflict in the first place, we allow ourselves to be pulled off the path to success in the bigger picture.

Imagine you are in a rush to pick up some whipped cream from the grocery store before friends arrive for your spouse's birthday celebration, when another car cuts in front of you and "steals" your parking space. If you remain focused on getting home to make a delectable strawberry shortcake, congratulations. But if you keep your engine idling while you wait for the other driver to get out of her car so you can confront her, you're falling right into the Need-to-Win Trap.

The best-case scenario is you convince her to get back in her car and give you the spot, or to admit that what she did was wrong (and the chance of either happening is very low). Meanwhile, the clock is ticking without care and your friends are arriving at the party, wondering where you are. Your need to win the silly conflict over a parking space is jeopardizing your objective for being there in the first place. That's a trap.

When a hockey player is fouled and then goes out of his way to retaliate on the next play, incurring a penalty that hurts the team, he's falling into the Need-to-Win Trap. He's allowing a small conflict with one person to distract him from the larger goal of winning the game. When a politician in a debate spends most of her time defending herself against accusations rather than addressing the crucial issues of the election, she's been pulled into the Need-to-Win Trap.

The path into the Need-to-Win Trap begins innocently enough. It can start when we set out to achieve a specific goal (*pick up something from the store*). Along the way, we encounter an obstacle we must overcome to achieve our goal (*get a parking space in a crowded lot*). Then at some point, a switch gets flipped, and the need to overcome the obstacle is no longer merely a means to achieve the original goal, but instead becomes the primary goal (*engage in conflict with a stranger over this parking space*).

When winning the short-term conflict becomes our primary objective, we stop looking for other avenues to accomplish our original task. Buying whipped cream takes a backseat to *winning this parking spot war*. Even if a better option were to present itself, we'd likely ignore it because we are driven by our need to win (*so we don't grab an even closer space that opens up*). That's when we know we are in the trap. Our emotions carry the conflict into destructive territory, where we waste time and adopt a "you versus me" mentality—all of which make resolving conflict more difficult.

If we aren't careful, we can become so focused on winning that we actually lose sight of the larger objective that started the whole thing. That's what happens to us in busy parking lots, and that's what happened to me in Judge Morcom's courtroom. My need to win the case nearly blinded me from a very advantageous settlement offer that achieved my primary goal of serving my client.

But wait, wasn't my desire to win the case exactly what put me in a position to get the settlement offer in the first place? This brings us to a very important consideration: how do we remain competitive without letting our emotions blind us from the big picture?

ISN'T IT GOOD TO BE COMPETITIVE?

Competition is a form of conflict that, like all conflict, can be healthy or toxic. It can be a great motivator that drives innovation, productivity, and the advancement of our species, but it can also distract us from our goals.

Part of what determines whether competitive conflicts are healthy or toxic is the context. For example, Adrian Amos, strong safety for the Green Bay Packers, tweeted in 2020: "I don't care if its spades or 2 on 2 basketball. If you on my team, we lose and your response is 'so it's just a game' I'll never play with you again." His coaches and teammates consider this obsession with winning to be a healthy mindset, and for NFL teams focused on winning football games, it is. But carrying that same mindset into a political discussion at the Thanksgiving dinner table will probably ruin the holiday for everyone.

To determine whether conflict would be productive, consider the ultimate goal. On the football field, the goal is to win the game, so an extremely competitive mindset is productive, not toxic. However, at the dinner table, the goal is to connect with loved ones and enjoy quality time together, so getting competitive about political disagreements is counterproductive.

Understanding someone's ultimate goal is critical to determining whether or not they're falling into the Need-to-Win Trap. This is a lesson I learned years ago when I represented a company in a complex lawsuit. The case was a messy commercial litigation (what lawyers call "business divorce"). There were multiple plaintiffs, defendants, crossclaims, counter-claims, and allegations going in every direction in a dizzying web of conflict. It was over the installation of a multi-million-dollar piece of machinery that needed to minimize vibrations in operation because...who frickin' cares? Bottom line: a deal went badly and everybody lawyered up.

While I understood the technical aspects of each claim, I couldn't figure out *why* the dispute was happening. What was the goal? Looking at the big picture, it didn't make sense. From a business perspective, this deal should have resolved long before it ended up in court. What was driving this conflict?

I called up Bert, my client, and told him I didn't understand why this situation hadn't already been resolved.

"I know what you're missing," he said, sounding like he was smiling on the other end of the phone. Then he started talking about Milton, the man who started the lawsuit (and, randomly, about golf):

"I love golf. I can't get enough of it. I don't like the country club crowd all that much, but I belong to one because it's got a great golf course. Litigation is Milton's version of golf. It's a sport to him. He's constantly suing people. He sued his business partner of twenty-five years. He sued his neighbor. He even sued his own brother! I've been doing business with Milton for years, and I guess it was my turn to get sued."

Everything about the case instantly made sense. Milton needed to win. All. The. Time. Worse than that, Milton needed to win by fighting. If the other side easily gave in to

Milton's demands without a fight, he would not be satisfied. Milton was what some people might call an asshole. Actually, I think *anyone* would call him an asshole.

Maybe you've encountered someone like Milton. Conflict swirls around these people like bees around honey. Dealing with Miltons can be exhausting. They tend to argue about everything and they never concede on a single issue. That puts a lot of strain on interactions they have with others. People like Milton would rather win than be happy. Milton himself was seventy-five years old, and any hope that he would suddenly decide to become a born-again reasonable person at that stage of life was desperately misplaced. His primary goal was simply to fight and win in court. (Later in this chapter, I'll offer some tactics for how to deal with the Miltons of the world.)

If winning serves your ultimate goal then you aren't falling into the Need-to-Win Trap (even if your goal is petty, as in Milton's case). In that case, you're just being competitive. It is only when the desire to defeat someone else pulls you away from your primary objective that it becomes problematic. That's what creates the Need-to-Win Trap.

If my client's ultimate goal in the lawsuit before Judge Morcum had been to hold the bus company publicly accountable for its deceit, we would have demanded a public apology. Accepting the settlement offer would have defeated the purpose of the lawsuit. But the ultimate goal wasn't to prove them wrong; it was to reimburse my client for her medical expenses and compensate her for her injuries. That's why my rejection of the defendant's offer was an example of the Need-to-Win Trap.

One of the best-known examples of someone with an obsessive need to win is Michael Jordan, who is still regarded by many as the best basketball player in the history of the game. (Take it easy, LeBron fans.) While Jordan was born with awesome raw talent, he never would have achieved his level of success had it not been for his unwavering commitment to winning. Michael Jordan worked harder and pushed himself more than almost any other player, and he demanded the same from his team. He was well known for being extremely harsh on his teammates in both practice and during games. In the 2020 documentary, *The Last Dance*, Jordan talked about how people may see him as a "tyrant" for the way he treated teammates.[21] He acknowledged that his unwavering commitment to winning affected his relationships decades later. Holding back tears, Jordan choked up as he gave an unapologetic explanation, "That's how I played the game. That was my mentality. If you don't want to play that way, don't play that way." Unlike Milton, Jordan is clearly pained by the lasting impact his need to win had on his relationships. But in the end, Jordan's goal was to win, so he did not fall into the Need-to-Win Trap. Everything he did was in service of his ultimate goal, even if he was insanely competitive.

Competition can motivate employees to work harder. But competition becomes toxic when it transforms from a healthy, fun-loving drive to an obsessive mindset. It can destroy teamwork and lead co-workers to sabotage each other. People fall into the Need-to-Win Trap when the switch gets flipped and

---

21 *The Last Dance*. 2020. Season 1, episode 7, "Episode VII." Directed by Jason Hehir. Aired May 10, 2020 on ESPN.

the need to win overtakes their primary goal. Let's look at the toxins that lead to the Need-to-Win Trap.

DRIVERS OF THE NEED TO WIN

The best way to teach you how to stay out of the Need-to-Win Trap is to describe how the trap works and why we fall into it so readily in the first place. The two toxins primarily responsible for the Need-to-Win Trap are ego and overinvestment. Let's break them down one at a time and investigate where they come from and why they can get out of control so easily.

Ego

The first driver of the Need-to-Win Trap is ego. Although the word often carries a negative connotation, as in *ego*centric or *ego*tistical, the ego actually includes both positive and negative aspects. On the positive side, ego refers to a solid, healthy sense of self. We all have ego. When we win at something, it makes us feel better about ourselves. Winning can build self-confidence.

But this can become problematic if our ego causes us to view winning as an identity, rather than an event. When you win, it makes you a *winner*. Winning is not just something you've done; it becomes who you are. The concept of ego is not limited to humans. In other species, from chimpanzees to antelope to beetles, winners of conflicts puff out their chests, strut around, and display signs of pleasure and confidence (yes, beetles strut). We have no way of knowing what they are thinking and feeling, but it looks a lot like ego. However, just because something exists in nature doesn't mean it's automatically healthy.

In both business and personal contexts, resolving a dispute with a mutually agreeable solution is usually the smart play. But it can *feel* like weakness, especially if the solution requires us to give in on a point we fiercely defended earlier. Capitulating can feel like a blow to our ego, and, therefore, to our identity. *Winners don't settle; they prevail at all costs.* It feels more satisfying to the ego if we can force someone else to bend to our will, rather than accommodate their needs. This toxic need to win is driven by emotion, not intellect.

During her contentious confirmation hearing to become President Trump's Secretary of Education, Betsy DeVos was asked to declare that guns should not be allowed in schools.[22] Not wanting to give any ammunition to gun control advocates *(sorry, couldn't resist the pun)*, she responded that guns were needed in schools to protect against grizzly bears. It was a ridiculous thing to say, and I'm sure she immediately regretted the comment, but her ego prevented her from correcting it. She never rescinded it, and the comment not only made the highlight reel of every late-night talk show, it became one of the focal points of the media's criticism over her qualifications. People tend to double down on comments they wish they hadn't made because of ego. We don't want to concede a point because we're afraid of looking weak. Ironically, this

---

22 "Full Committee Hearing Nomination of Betsy DeVos to serve as Secretary of Education," January 17, 2017. United States Senate Hearings Archive. https://www.help.senate.gov/hearings/nomination-of-betsy-devos-to-serve-as-secretary-of-education. Accessed on October 18, 2021.

stubbornness actually makes us weaker. Someone debating Betsy DeVos could continually attack that comment, pulling her into the Need-to-Win Trap and forcing her into a defensive position.

A toxic level of ego leads us into the Need-to-Win Trap when it causes us to double down on obvious mistakes or remain committed to an unproductive course of action because we're afraid of looking weak. That's what happened to Betsy DeVos: toxic ego committed her to a silly statement and kept her from correcting it and moving on to a more productive dialogue.

Toxic ego is also unproductive when it feeds our identity as a "winner." In the Judge Morcum case, I felt powerful, which fed my ego and kept me focused on winning. This further amped up my feelings of self-righteousness and gave me the audacity to appoint myself as the champion who would expose the bus company's lies. That, of course, wasn't my job. As Judge Morcum pointed out, my goal was to achieve the best possible result for my client. Toxic ego distracted me from accepting the bus company's settlement offer, which was a much better option for my client.

Overinvestment

The second main driver of the Need-to-Win Trap involves a toxin we haven't covered yet: overinvestment. This is defined by situations in which we continue a behavior in an attempt to recoup previously invested resources. Psychologists label this the *Sunk Cost Fallacy*. Studies show we have a harder time giving something up after we've invested time, money, effort, or other resources in it.

For example, we might order too much food at a restaurant and then overeat just to *get our money's worth*. (I am definitely guilty of this one.) Similarly, a person who bought expensive concert tickets may drive for hours through a blizzard even though he is sick with a cold on the day of the event, because he has to justify the initial investment of buying the tickets by forcing himself to try to have a good time. Overinvestment can cause us to stick with the original plan even when it no longer serves us. Because, damn it, we've already come this far.

The Sunk Cost Fallacy can lead to negative conflict when we apply it to human interaction. I was at lunch with my friend Brian recently and he ordered a hamburger with no tomato. When his burger came with a tomato, he simply took it off. Later, the waiter asked how everything was, and Brian said his burger was great but he ordered it with no tomato, as he was pointing to the discarded tomato on his plate.

"You didn't say 'no tomato,'" the waiter said, "I would've remembered that."

"I definitely said no tomato," Brian replied, "because I've been ordering hamburgers that way for my entire life."

Their back and forth continued and it got a little uncomfortable. With each passing second, Brian became more invested in the argument and less able to drop it. Soon, he wasn't going to stop until the waiter admitted he made a mistake—an acknowledgment Brian hadn't even cared about sixty seconds earlier. Brian wasted time and energy debating the tomato issue because overinvestment had pulled him into the Need-to-Win Trap. The waiter eventually took responsibility, but I don't think he believed it. Obviously, this trap has far greater consequences when dealing with something more important than an unloved tomato.

At car lots, one of the top strategies used by sales associates is to take up as much of a prospect's time as possible. While this might seem like terrible customer service, the psychology behind the approach makes sense. The more time you invest interacting with a certain sales rep, the less inclined you will feel to leave and buy your car from someone else.

Overinvestment and ego can feed each other. I mentioned earlier that I've fallen victim to the Sunk Cost Fallacy when ordering too much food. On a subconscious level, I'm embarrassed for over ordering, so I'll eat all of it just to prove I didn't make a mistake. That's ego. The ridiculous part is that sometimes I'm proving it to someone I'll never see again (like the waiter). This is a silly example, but when this dynamic plays out in a more serious context, it can lead to destructive results. For example, you can imagine what might have happened if Judge Morcum hadn't pulled me out of the Need-to-Win Trap. I had invested significant effort in my plan to set a trap for the bus driver and spring it on him in front of the jury, and I didn't want that effort to go to waste.

Even in a casual debate with a friend or loved one, backing off from our position can be a tough pill to swallow—and the absurdity is that it might be a position we don't even care much about. People have confided in me that they've found themselves vigorously defending an argument they don't care about simply because they invested effort in the argument, and their ego drove them to continue. The good news is that some of those same people reported back to me that once they learned to identify the toxins, they were able to avoid the Need-to-Win Trap.

STOPPING THE CYCLE

It's better to be proactive than reactive. Understanding the drivers of the Need-to-Win Trap is important because it is easier to spot these toxins as they build and avoid the trap at the outset than it is to pull yourself out of the trap after you've already fallen in.

We all are hardwired with fight or flight responses to conflict; that's a billion years of evolution at work. In the jungle, those responses save lives. But at the negotiating table or in a business interaction, those instinctive emotions can drive an extremely poor outcome.

If you find yourself feeling physiological responses to conflict—the hair on the back of your neck standing up or your respiration speeding up—stop. Take a beat. Ask yourself, *Am I falling into one of the Conflict Traps? Is the person I'm dealing with falling into one?* Simply asking these questions will pull you out of an instinctive response and into intellectual awareness. That presence of mind gives you power and control. Once you stop the cycle, you can apply some effective tools.

Catering to Ego

Here's a negotiating tip: catering to your own ego is very costly, but catering to someone else's is free. If you find yourself dealing with a person whose ego is driving conflict, feed that person's ego. It will cost you nothing. Recognize that she needs to feel powerful. So tell her she's powerful and respectfully ask that she not use her power to hurt you. Of course, put that in your own words. If you are perceived as condescending or manipulative, you will humiliate the other person and make your job harder. The goal is to stop both your ego *and* her ego from elevating to toxic levels.

We can't fully detox our ego until we gain the ability to recognize when it is driving our behavior and proactively pump the brakes. You will get better at identifying when your ego is driving a conflict in real time with practice. You can learn the habit of creating a mental space that allows you to momentarily step outside of a situation and view it more objectively.

Sometimes you might even realize your ego is driving a conflict and decide it's worth it. You might tell yourself, *I'm going to pay the price to feed my ego because it will feel good.* Knowingly catering to your ego might not be the best interim step, but it's certainly better than *unknowingly* catering to it.

Once you notice how often your ego is driving your behavior, you will begin to see the same phenomenon at play in others, too. This is when you ask: *Is my ego driving my behavior? Is the other person's ego driving theirs?* Merely asking these questions will raise your level of awareness. When you become adept at asking these questions in real time during conflict, you will see the other person's ego as a resource that is available to you. You can use it to your advantage.

When I was working as an executive at ePrize, I learned to proactively manage the egos of corporate lawyers in order to make conference calls more efficient and close deals faster.

When we were building our digital promotions company, we had seventy-five of the world's top one hundred brands among our clients. These are massive corporations with thousands of employees and steaming piles of bureaucracy. We spent a lot of time on absurdly inefficient conference calls. This means the kind where the first ten minutes of the call are spent waiting for all the right people to dial-in, and then everyone spends a couple more minutes talking about why they were late: *Whoever set up the conference call invited the wrong Lisa; Bob went to the wrong conference room; Jen was stuck on another conference call that went long; Cheryl kept entering the wrong password....* By the time everyone had introduced themselves, we'd be fortunate to get fifteen minutes of actual work done in a one-hour call.

But I digress.

On one of these conference calls, I was working with a lawyer in our client's legal department who was pushing for changes that I believed were problematic. This meant there would be an audience listening to us negotiate each point. Ego inevitably kicked in, causing the lawyer to dig in on his position—even at times when he realized he'd made a mistake—because he needed to save face in front of his co-workers—nobody wants to look bad in front of an audience. From the lawyer's perspective, the goal of reaching the best solution for the project took a back seat to catering to his own ego. Calls would often end without resolution, requiring a series of follow up emails and more mind-numbing conference calls. This, in turn, led to delays, compressed timelines, and working conditions that shifted into tense urgency and, ultimately, all-out crisis. Say hello to toxic conflict.

I decided to try a different approach.

The day before one of these big conference calls, I called the lawyer on the other side to go over his proposed changes in advance. I began by complimenting him on one of the changes he'd made that was an improvement over my team's work: "That's actually a great way to handle this issue, and I hope you don't mind if I steal that and use it for other projects moving forward." This wasn't a manipulation tactic; it was the truth, and it had the added benefit of feeding his ego. After receiving the respect he wanted, the lawyer was open to hearing why some of his other changes created issues we wanted to avoid. I acknowledged that he had a difficult job, complimented him on his work, and asked for his help in reaching a solution for the benefit of his company. In other words, I fed his ego so it would not later rise to toxic levels and create unhealthy conflict.

The following day, the conference call was smooth sailing. I made a point to publicly thank him for improving our work. Their lawyer got to shine in front of his coworkers, and we hashed through our differences of opinion in a productive dialogue. When I brought up the points I needed to make, he backed me up and vice versa. Our collaborative approach set the tone for others on the call as well. There were no petty arguments or emotional ultimatums, and everyone worked toward solutions. Catering to the lawyer's ego neutralized its toxic effects, allowing us to move forward and progress toward our collective goals. The end result is that we engaged in

healthy conflict and quickly arrived at solutions for the benefit of the project.

After that, I used this approach on every future conference
call with consistent success. Catering to someone's ego can
detox interactions and enable both sides to embrace conflict
in a healthy way.

Cut Your Losses on Overinvestment

Overinvestment and ego tend to work hand in hand. In the
same way self-awareness of our ego detoxes its negative effects,
acceptance of our overinvestments does the same. There's no
magic here; it is as simple as it sounds. If you bought expensive concert tickets but you're sick on the night of the event,
you shouldn't attend. What's done is done. Suffering through
a miserable evening as a justification for your financial investment simply makes a bad situation worse. Better to cut
your losses.

The same applies to emotional investments. If you get
into an argument with a friend but your passion wanes after
a half-hour and you start to regret engaging in the first place,
that's a good time to call it quits. But letting go at this point
is difficult because part of you is preoccupied with the thirty
minutes you've invested with nothing to show for it—you
have not won the argument yet. It might not be obvious in
the heat of the moment, but the mere fact that you have been
at it for thirty minutes is a bad reason to continue if you no
longer care about the argument. That would be an irrational
justification for the emotional investment. It's better to cut
your losses.

The only way to detox the effect of overinvestment is to accept it.

When you recognize you've fallen victim to the Sunk Cost Fallacy and are chasing a loss, it becomes easy to step back and assess whether overinvestment is driving your need to win. If so, cut your losses.

DEALING WITH MILTONS

Let's revisit the Milton example from earlier. We've all encountered a Milton at one time or another. Miltons are people who simply need to win all the time. From Milton's perspective, he never needs to worry about falling into the Need-to-Win Trap because winning is his *only* goal. The problem is that people like Milton tend to have a gravitational pull that lures others into the Need-to-Win Trap. Unless your goal, like Milton's, is to fight and win at all costs, it's best to steer clear of these people. However, sometimes they are unavoidable. One of the more extreme conflicts a Milton can pull you into is a lawsuit.

The first key to dealing with someone like Milton is to simply accept him for who he is. Don't take it personally, and don't think you can convince him to change. Once we accept the nature of someone like Milton, our options become clear: give him what he wants, push for a fair settlement, or go to war. Ideally, we will select whichever option costs the least amount of money, but there are other factors to consider. Lawsuits are stressful. They drain mental and emotional energy. It may be *worth it* to settle and avoid the stress.

Sometimes we fight hard for our principles. However, in my experience, most people soften their stance once they realize how much their principles are costing them in legal fees. The point is that when we accept that someone like Milton is constantly pulling others into the Need-to-Win Trap, we can keep ourselves out of the trap and dispassionately decide on a course of action.

But what about dealing with someone like Milton outside of litigation? What if you have to work with a Milton or are related to one? The analysis is still the same. Accept that the person will not change, clarify the options, and select the one that costs the least. Oftentimes, this *cost* will not be in dollars, but rather in stress, the regret of softening your principles, or lost peace of mind.

You must view your options in the context of the length of the relationship and its value to you. Is this a person you only need to deal with for a short period of time? Is this a lifelong relationship? Is this someone you're forced to work with, your next-door neighbor, or your mother-in-law? Depending on the nature of the relationship, the costs and your tolerance for those costs will vary.

Once you've accepted that the person won't change, you can decide whether this a relationship you want to preserve. If so, how much effort (i.e. cost) are you willing to put into maintaining it? See Chapter 7, Don't Get Mad at Penguins Because They Can't Fly, for a deep dive into how we can detox conflict with people who will not change.

The good news is that there are relatively few Miltons in the world. Most people aren't hypercompetitive by nature, but we all sometimes get caught up in the need to beat someone at something or to prove others wrong.

Overall, the best philosophy for avoiding the Need-to-Win Trap is to raise your level of awareness. The tools covered above make that a manageable task. Toxic levels of ego and overinvestment create optimal conditions for the Need-to-Win Trap. Remember the questions to ask when you find yourself feeling the physiological effects of conflict: *Am I falling into one of the Conflict Traps? Is the person I'm dealing with falling into one?* Merely asking the questions will go a long way toward breaking the cycle.

Take note of your ego—as well as the other person's ego—and decide whether any amount of ego is driving the conflict. If you realize the other person's ego is at play, be grateful to have a tool at your disposal that costs you nothing: feed that person's ego. If your own ego is the issue, decide whether to allow that to continue or not. And don't forget about the Sunk Cost Fallacy! Overinvestment can influence you to follow through with plans that no longer serve your original goal.

Next, we're going to look at what could be considered the opposite problem of the Need-to-Win Trap: the Avoidance Trap. In Chapter 4, we'll explore the inner workings of SEAL Team 6, the Pampers diapers packages with swear words printed on them, and much more.

UNDERSTANDING THE NEED-TO-WIN TRAP

Winning can be a distraction

When your desire to beat someone else causes you to lose sight of your larger goal, you have fallen into the Need-to-Win Trap.

Emotion can be a weakness

We often rely on feelings of anger or self-righteousness to build ourselves up into feeling powerful but, in fact, these emotions can be our greatest weaknesses.

Two Toxins that Lead to the Need-to-Win Trap

- Ego: The need to feed our ego can cause us to fight harder and longer even when doing so no longer serves our larger goal. Reaching a compromise with someone else can feel like losing or weakness, so our ego pushes us to win, not settle. The other person's ego can drive them in the same way.

- Overinvestment: We have a harder time giving something up after we've invested time, money, effort, or other resources in it. This is the Sunk Cost Fallacy, which describes our desire to continue pursuing a goal to recoup our investment even when doing so is no longer in our best interest.

TOOLS TO OVERCOME THE NEED-TO-WIN TRAP

Notice the signs
Learn to be aware of when your need to win is being triggered so you can stop yourself from getting pulled into the trap.

Catering to your own ego is costly, but catering to someone else's is free
When you feel the physiological effects of conflict, ask yourself: Is my ego driving my behavior? Is the other person's ego driving their behavior?

- If your ego is driving the conflict, hit the pause button. Make an intellectual decision as to whether you want to continue; don't let your ego drive your behavior.
- If you see that the other person's ego is driving the conflict, feed that person's ego. It will cost you nothing.

Cut your losses on overinvestment
When you find yourself pursuing a goal because you've already invested so much, it is easy to assess whether overinvestment is driving your need to win. If so, cut your losses.

Accept the nature of a Milton
If you're dealing with someone who needs to win all the time, don't get pulled into the trap for the sake of competition. Instead, accept that the person will not change, clarify your options, and select the one that costs the least.

CHAPTER 4

The Avoidance Trap

Conflict is inevitable, and when we attempt to avoid it we usually make things worse. Fail to address an issue and you give it a chance to fester and escalate. The Avoidance Trap—the most common of the four Conflict Traps—occurs when we avoid a conflict because of toxic fear. In the context of the fight-or-flight reflex, this is *flight*. When fear reaches toxic levels, it prevents us from asking questions, admitting mistakes, offering ideas, or calling out problems. Toxic fear causes us to run from conflict rather than embrace it for success. This emotion is the primary driver of the Avoidance Trap.

A stark example is the General Motors ignition switch crisis covered in Chapter 1. While that began as a technical problem, the company's failure to address the issue allowed it to escalate into a tragic loss of human life. Billions of dollars were wasted, public trust was shattered, and the company faced one of the worst crises since its founding over one hundred years ago. That was a corporate culture with a severe aversion to conflict, and they paid a devastating price.

While General Motors is an extreme case, there are many scenarios that can lead into the Avoidance Trap. If you had food in your teeth, would you want someone to tell you before you walked into a big meeting? Of course you would. However, when the situation is reversed, it can be uncomfortable to point this type of thing out to someone else. That discomfort prevents most people from saying anything; we avoid the conflict. The irony is that the embarrassment of learning about the food in your teeth before the meeting is nothing compared to the embarrassment of looking in the mirror afterward and realizing it's been there all day. Avoiding a small conflict often does more harm in the long run. A bit of spinach may seem trivial compared to the devastating consequences experienced by General Motors, but the mechanics of how the Avoidance Trap works are the same. Consider some other scenarios:

> A carpenter on a construction site notices the protective coating on some electrical wiring has been torn away, exposing wires that are pressed against a wooden beam. The wiring has already been approved by the city inspector (after a two-week delay), and a drywall crew is five minutes away from sealing the exposed wires in the wall, hiding them forever. The carpenter has no electrical training so he isn't sure whether this presents a risk, and he knows waiting for an electrician to come back to the site would delay the project, which is already behind schedule and over budget, so he walks away without saying anything.

An employee at a marketing agency sends a tweet from her personal account criticizing a major brand's ad campaign. A week later, that same brand becomes her new client. She thinks about "coming clean" and telling the client about the tweet. However, knowing the tweet is already a week old and thinking that the odds of the client finding it diminish with each passing day, she decides to avoid the difficult conversation.

A nurse on the night shift at a hospital notices the dosage for a particular patient seems high. She considers calling the doctor at home to check the order, but recalls the doctor's disparaging comments about her abilities the last time she called him at home. She decides that since the dosage is clearly indicated on the chart, it must be correct, so she proceeds to administer the medication.[23]

Each of these scenarios has the potential to end badly, and they are all examples of behavior motivated by toxic fear. It's easy to think that if we were in any one of these situations we would behave differently. We would do the right thing and have the difficult conversation. But the truth is that most of us regularly avoid conflict in our daily lives.

The Avoidance Trap often shows up in the context of personal relationships. Instead of explaining to our friend, family member, or romantic partner exactly how their behavior

---

23 Example presented by Amy Edmondson in her TedxHGSE Talk on April 12, 2014. Uploaded to YouTube May 5, 2014. https://www. youtube.com/watch?v=LhoLuui9gX8. Accessed October 19, 2021.

bothers us, we don't say anything because we don't want to seem rude. We drop small hints but don't directly lay out what we'd like others to do differently.

Imagine you have a good friend who is genuinely supportive, but you notice that when you share good news, he often makes a subtle reference to a past mistake or a time when you failed. These comments inject negativity into your happy moments, and you don't like it. It's easy to talk yourself out of saying something to your friend about his behavior. After all, you don't want to make the issue a bigger deal than it is. He might not even be aware he's doing it, and the risk of appearing confrontational or offending him is enough to stop most of us from saying anything. We tell ourselves our silence is based on respect, but it's actually based on fear of an uncomfortable conversation.

Remaining silent is disrespectful to the relationship. If you don't explain how the comments make you feel and address the issue together, you may grow resentful of your friend and the relationship can suffer over time. The fear of offending someone in the short term often causes us to avoid small conflicts, which can lead to much bigger problems later on. That is the Avoidance Trap in action. Confronting your friend about his comments might be uncomfortable in the moment, but if you can do it in a non-accusatory way (this would be an excellent use of the Shopping List Voice) your relationship will ultimately be stronger as a result.

THREE TOXIC FEAR FACTORS

There are three sources of toxic fear that can lead into the Avoidance Trap: lack of psychological safety, impression management, and socialization. Sometimes they work independently and other times they work in combination with one another.

These three factors were all at play in the case of the General Motors ignition switch story. The real tragedy in the case of GM is that a small handful of people inside the company knew—for more than ten years—that they were putting defective ignition switches into cars, but they said nothing. How does that happen? How can compassionate human beings turn a blind eye to a problem that ultimately killed 124 people? They were in flight mode. We instinctively run from conflict. It *feels* safer to run than to engage. In fact, most people will avoid a small immediate conflict even if it sends us running toward a larger conflict later on. This isn't rational, but it's instinctive. When we are in a culture that discourages bad news or contradictory opinions, the energy and courage required to swim upstream against that current is greater than the energy it takes to keep quiet and hope for the best. The larger the organization, the bigger the problem because it takes more energy to speak up against the status quo. No one wants to be the one to suggest the company recall thousands of cars, incur massive expense, tarnish its reputation, and drive its stock price down. In a conflict-avoidant culture, it's easier to do nothing and hide in the crowd. If bad things eventually happen, the blame can be spread around. None of this is deliberate—it is the mindset of toxic fear.

The first factor that drives toxic fear is a lack of psychological safety. Amy Edmondson, an organizational behavioral scientist at Harvard, defines this as "a belief that one will not be punished or humiliated for speaking up with ideas, questions, concerns, or mistakes."[24] In organizations that lack psychological safety, fear can elevate to toxic levels that lead directly into the Avoidance Trap. If we discover a problem (like a defective ignition switch that can kill people), the rational response is to speak up and work with others in our organization to fix it. But if we are afraid we'll be punished or humiliated for calling out a mistake, our defense mechanisms kick in and override that rational response. We feel the impulse to run from confrontation, which is easy when all we have to do is keep quiet.

The second toxic fear factor that can lead to the Avoidance Trap is the urge to control how we are perceived by others—a trait psychologists refer to as *impression management*. Most of us are not confronted with high-stakes situations like the GM ignition switch, but we all would like to be viewed as smart, capable, and likable. Certainly no one wants to come across as ignorant, incompetent, intrusive, or negative (which are legitimate fears for anyone in a culture that lacks psychological safety). Professor Edmondson points out how easy it can be to manage this fear. If you don't want to look ignorant, simply don't ask questions; if you don't want to appear incompetent, don't admit mistakes or ask for help; if you don't want to

---

24 Ibid.

intrude, don't offer ideas; and if you don't want to be viewed as negative, don't critique the status quo.[25]

When fear prevents people from asking questions, admitting mistakes, offering ideas, or calling out problems, it is *toxic*. Try to imagine an organization in which people don't ask questions, challenge ideas, give constructive criticism, venture outside their comfort zone, sound the alarm if they see a threat, or engage in uncomfortable-but-important conversations. That is almost certain to be an unhealthy organization that lacks innovation; is a weak competitor in its market; does not develop strong leaders; and has a hard time attracting and retaining talent. Those are some of the many consequences of the Avoidance Trap. Before Mary Barra took over as GM's CEO and changed the culture, the company suffered from several of these problems.

In addition to a lack of psychological safety and impression management, socialization is the third toxic fear factor that can lead to the Avoidance Trap. Chapter 1 reviewed how we are socialized from a young age to soften bad news and sugarcoat feedback. We're told, *If you don't have anything nice to say, don't say anything at all.* We are taught to be respectful, agreeable, and polite, which of course is very good advice (sometimes). However, when these lessons cause us to shy away from uncomfortable, yet important, issues, those issues go unaddressed. Over time, they can fester into more serious problems.

---

25 Ibid.

WHAT'S WRONG WITH AVOIDANCE?

You may be wondering, *Isn't it tactful to avoid conflict?* After all, if you go around calling out every little issue, you're a confrontational jerk, right? Not exactly. While there are plenty of situations in which avoiding conflict is the healthy choice and will not lead you into the Avoidance Trap, there are just as many instances in which running from conflict is a bad move. The main difference lies in the motivation behind the avoidance. The Avoidance Trap is driven by toxic fear. When we choose to avoid a conflict for a reason other than toxic fear, we are not falling into the trap. Put another way, we need to pick our battles.

For an example of non-toxic fear, imagine that another driver just cut in front of you in the parking lot at the mall and "stole" your parking space. Maybe you're having a rough week and you've been taken advantage of one too many times lately. Your temper flares and you step out of the car to tell that parking space thief to relinquish the spot to you. But then you see the other driver; he's a 6' 5" bodybuilder with "I've Killed for Less" tattooed on his chest and a gun rack on the back of his monster truck. The rush of fear you feel in that moment isn't toxic; it's a genuine survival instinct. Confronting this guy is not a good idea. Giving in to that fear will *not* lead you into the Avoidance Trap; it will lead you to safety. You can take solace in the fact that he definitely needed that parking space more than you did. Get back into your car and go find another spot.

We also choose to avoid conflict when fear is not part of the equation at all. Imagine you have a colleague at work who continually takes credit for other people's ideas, including your own. You are concerned that some of your valuable contributions will go unnoticed by your leader, whose opinion matters when it comes to raises and promotions. You are not afraid of confronting the colleague; in fact, you would get real satisfaction from doing so. But you are aware of two additional factors: first, that the leaders in your company, including your boss, are aware of your colleague's manipulative tactics and his future at the company is limited; and second, that he will never acknowledge his bad behavior, and confronting him will make it difficult to work with him going forward. So you avoid the conflict not out of fear, but because the cost-benefit analysis makes it not worth your time. You've decided *not to get mad at penguins because they can't fly*, which is the focus of Chapter 7. Again, it is only when toxic fear drives your behavior that you are slipping into the Avoidance Trap.

If we are honest with ourselves, most of us can think back over the past few weeks and identify a time when concerns over psychological safety, impression management, or socialization kept us silent. Maybe you noticed a problem and knew how to fix it but held your tongue to avoid getting yelled at. Or perhaps you had a question about something but didn't ask because you figured maybe you should already know. Or you may have seen someone make a mistake but chose not to address it out of fear of offending him. We are all guilty of Avoidance—it's human nature. But every time we stay silent, we deprive ourselves and those around us of the ability to uncover and fix problems, and to learn and grow as people. We deprive our organizations of opportunities to innovate, compete, and advance.

AVOIDANCE HURTS

Running from conflict can cause all kinds of problems in our personal lives. When we hide our true feelings from others, it cuts off honest communication and eliminates the opportunity for open dialogue. Conflicts remain unresolved, and so do the toxic feelings associated with them. As these toxins build up, small issues grow into larger ones. The resulting stress can reduce our ability to concentrate, remember things, make decisions, learn, and interact with others. By avoiding conflicts, we suppress our feelings and bottle up our frustration, which can lead to stress-related physical ailments like ulcers, migraines, and back pain. Chronic stress from unresolved conflicts can also weaken the immune system, making us more susceptible to illnesses like the common cold. All of these ailments further reduce our resilience to stress, making it more likely that we will continue to avoid conflict in the future. This feeds a vicious cycle from one Avoidance Trap to another.

In addition to creating personal problems, the avoidance of conflict can lead to systemic problems on an organizational level. In the case of General Motors, once the ignition switch defect was discovered, the company faced two options. Option one, it could engage with the conflict head on by publicly announcing the defect and initiating a proactive recall of all affected vehicles. Or option two, it could avoid the problem until it escalated to the point where it was impossible to avoid, and *then* initiate a recall of all affected vehicles. One of these options involves billions more dollars in fines than the other, and the loss of many lives (hint: it's option two—avoiding the problem). GM chose the costlier option because it was stuck in the Avoidance Trap.

In a conflict avoidance culture, people not only avoid taking action, they avoid even thinking through the consequences of inaction. This type of culture keeps everyone focused on *impression management*. People in these organizations allow problems to remain hidden out of fear that sounding the alarm will negatively impact their careers, or even get them fired. Unfortunately, this is a valid fear in many corporate cultures, including GM.

Some have argued that the problem with GM's culture was simply that the company prioritized profit over safety. But that explanation is too simplistic and falls apart upon examination. An early recall actually would have been a cheaper solution. By waiting, they ultimately paid billions more in fines, legal settlements, investigations, and public relations. If all GM cared about was the bottom line, it would have blown the whistle on the ignition switch defect right away. The real cause of the crisis was not a focus on profit, it was a toxic corporate culture that pulled GM employees into the Avoidance Trap.

When Mary Barra took over as CEO, she detoxed the culture from top to bottom. She instituted things like the "Speak Up" alert discussed in Chapter 1, which made it easy for an assembly line worker who saw that a part was installed incorrectly to "speak up" and raise the issue. Employees no longer needed to muster up Herculean levels of courage to call out problems. Avoidance was easy before because the culture encouraged it. The new detoxed culture at GM celebrated speaking up, which then encouraged everyone to seek out opportunities to voice concerns.

The good news is, you don't have to be a world class CEO like Mary Barra to detox conflict. There are some simple, straightforward things we all can do to stay out of the Avoidance Trap.

AVOIDING THE AVOIDANCE TRAP

Now that we have identified what the Avoidance Trap looks like (running from conflict) and what causes it (toxic fear), the rest of this chapter will focus on two methods for cleansing toxic fear from our organizations and minds, which will keep the Avoidance Trap from ensnaring us. The first tool is to make conflict a requirement. The second is to promote a culture of candor and accountability. Let's examine these ideas one at a time.

Don't Avoid Conflict; Require It

The Navy SEALs have an easy solution to the problem of toxic fear. For the SEALs, strong communication is a life-or-death necessity. On the battlefield, avoiding an awkward conversation can put lives at risk. SEALs have to speak up whenever they notice a problem. They can't worry about hurting each other's feelings. So, how do they train their soldiers to communicate without toxic fear?

I had the honor of learning the SEALs' communication methods from Matt Bissonnette, who was a member of SEAL Team 6 during the Osama bin Laden raid and later became the leader of SEAL Team 6. Before he came into the room, we were asked to put our phones away so that no one could take photographs of Matt. His appearance is kept secret because there are people out there who would come for him and his family if they figured out his civilian identity.

"You guys in the business world suck at communication," Matt told us. He had come to speak to a group of leaders at our company about tactics to create a culture that encourages open communication. I expected him to do what all corporate speakers do: give us a simple five-step framework we could use to communicate better (kind of like what I'm doing in this book). But instead, Matt told a story about his first mission as leader of SEAL Team 6.

The team was in the middle of the mission when Matt's commanding officer radioed from base, asking when to send the helicopter for a pick up. Matt radioed back that they would be wrapping up in about ten minutes. (I have no idea what they were doing on this mission, but rest assured, it was some badass SEAL Team stuff.) He then checked in with the new guy to make sure he still had the ladder (apparently this mission required the use of a ladder, and the new guy always has to carry the ladder). The new guy confirmed he had the ladder, and ten minutes later, they were all on the helicopter heading back to base.

After every mission, the SEALs have a mandatory debrief meeting to talk about what went well, what didn't go well, and share feedback. Importantly, there is always time at the end of the meeting for anyone to say anything they want.

"I've got a question," said the new guy. "Why'd you radio me and ask if I still had my ladder?"

Matt was surprised by the question and his first impulse was to respond with, "BECAUSE I'M THE LEADER OF SEAL TEAM 6, AND I'LL ASK YOU WHATEVER THE HELL I WANT AND YOU WILL ANSWER, THAT'S WHY." But he resisted that impulse and gave a more diplomatic answer along the lines of, "I didn't mean anything by it; we were getting ready to head out and I just wanted to make sure everyone had their gear."

The new guy didn't let it go. "You know, that ladder weighs about seventy pounds and I had to carry it while we were running through the mountains for two-and-a-half hours on the way to this mission. Did you think I was going to forget it and not realize I didn't have it with me? I didn't ask whether you remembered your assault rifle. You were giving me shit because I'm the new guy."

Matt realized he'd been micromanaging and had demonstrated poor leadership. He immediately owned up to it, took responsibility, apologized, and thanked the new guy for bringing it up. Matt told us it was a good thing the new guy had felt safe enough to make this comment, because that sort of thing can be habit forming. If this behavior had gone unchecked, Matt might have radioed the new guy toward the end of every mission after that to make sure he had his ladder. This would have pissed the guy off and created resentment, which eventually would have led to a serious problem. Think about going on a SEAL Team mission and putting your life in someone else's hands.... Do you want that person to resent you? If the new guy had kept silent out of fear of confronting Matt—if he had run away from the small conflict—it could have sent them both down a path toward a much larger conflict at some point in the future. His fear could have turned to resentment and anger, and they would have fallen into the Avoidance Trap.

This story ties back to the Bully Trap, covered in Chapter 2, and shows how the Bully Trap can lead into the Avoidance Trap. Not only was it critical that the new guy embraced conflict by confronting Matt during the meeting, but Matt's response was equally important. If Matt had acted on his first impulse to yell at the new guy, it would have shut down communication and discouraged everyone else on the team from calling out issues in the future. That type of bullying behavior can encourage subversive tactics like manipulation, undermining, and finger pointing, and creates resentment and disloyalty.

When interpersonal problems go unaddressed and are allowed to fester, they can grow into something much worse. For a Navy SEAL, this might even mean that in the heat of battle, the person protecting you is someone who harbors resentment toward you. That's not a recipe for a successful mission. So, it's important for Navy SEALs to address issues head on with candor, rather than avoiding difficult conversations.

The SEALS use a "mandatory debrief" after each mission, and this is a great tactic for combating the Avoidance Trap in civilian cultures as well. This is a procedure that requires confrontation and conflict. The US military is generally a top-down, command-and-control organization. Questioning a superior officer is a big deal and requires tremendous strength and courage—even more than questioning your boss does in the business world. But Navy SEALs know that in order to be effective as a team, they must question, contradict, and openly confront one another. They cannot afford to operate in a culture that requires strength and courage merely to speak one's mind. The SEALs understand that non-toxic conflict is a necessary component of a healthy team.

The same strategy can be used in business. It's a simple but effective tool: hold regularly scheduled debrief meetings or set aside time for debriefing within an existing meeting. This is a time when people are *required* to raise issues, call out problems, and get things off their chests. During a mandatory debrief, people aren't doing their jobs if they remain silent. Speaking up is everyone's duty.

There are two keys to making debrief meetings successful. First, stress the fact that speaking up is a job requirement. When you specifically designate a time for people to think critically about the organization and call out problems, you send the message that voicing concerns is a desired behavior. Sometimes people don't raise issues because they don't want the social stigma of being the source of conflict. No one wants to be *that guy*. Recall the *impression management* phenomenon referenced at the beginning of this chapter and how it encourages people to remain silent as a mechanism to manage the fear of appearing negative or incompetent. Debrief meetings redirect *impression management* to encourage speaking up; people who call out weaknesses or problems in the organization are now seen as helpful. Instead, it's those who remain silent who come across as dead weight that the rest of the organization needs to carry. If people don't want the stigma of remaining silent in these meetings, they will feel pressure to think hard about potential problems in the organization and will be motivated to speak up. That kind of pressure is productive and drives a healthy organization. Debrief meetings provide the psychological safety people need in order to speak up.

The second key to getting the most out of debrief meetings is to frame them as learning exercises, instead of execution problems. Here's a script to set the stage for a debrief session:

> "We each have a unique perspective that the group can benefit from, and some of you have identified weaknesses or obstacles that the rest of us haven't seen. It's important that everyone has a voice in this room because no one individual can have all the answers. Let's share our observations and concerns so we can learn as a team."

Emphasizing the debrief as a learning exercise helps people view an organization's weaknesses or issues with coworkers from an academic perspective. It puts psychological distance between an individual and the issues that cause discomfort. It teaches everyone that the organization is a psychologically safe environment.

In addition to a debrief, you can do one better and have a pre-brief meeting, too. Before embarking on a project, gather the group to discuss potential challenges, asking, "Let's assume we fail in this project; what would've caused that?" This puts even more psychological distance between the participants and potential problems. In this setting, people are free to creatively think about potential weaknesses in their organization or team without concern of offending others, because they are not being critical of things that have already happened. Everything is hypothetical and abstract, so it's less emotional.

Regularly occurring debrief and pre-brief meetings accomplish three things:

1. They provide continual opportunities to uncover problems in the organization and, therefore, bad news surfaces faster;

2. they engender a psychologically safe environment that gets people comfortable with confronting issues head on (people are freed from the social stigma of being the source of conflict and feel positive pressure to identify hidden problems and opportunities); and

3. they motivate and empower people to continually seek improvement.

Once this behavior is established in an organization through the context of these meetings, people will gravitate toward embracing conflict outside of the formal meetings as well. It simply becomes part of the culture.

Candor and Accountability

The second strategy for combating the Avoidance Trap is to instill a culture of candor and accountability within your organization. When done successfully, team members will feel safe speaking their minds and will encourage one another to share critical feedback. *Candor* is about saying the truth, even when it's awkward. *Accountability* is about admitting your own mistakes freely and openly, and holding others to account for their own errors.

How do you instill these two qualities within your organization? Let's cover candor first. An open dialogue is critical to the success of any organization. Regardless of whether we're in a business, non-profit, sports team, or any other group, we must address the obstacles confronting us *as a team*. Any organization that is weighed down by the need to tiptoe around difficult issues because *John is overly sensitive* or *Greg cries whenever you give him feedback* will lose. People in those organizations waste untold energy battling toxins that slow things down, rather than achieving goals. They squander resources on toxic conflict, while organizations with cultures of candor blow right past them.

The best way to instill candor into your culture is to practice it. *A lot.* When candid communication is rare in an organization, it takes real courage to engage in it. But when candor is practiced every day, it becomes effortless. Debrief and prebrief meetings are great opportunities to start conditioning people to speak with candor. Leaders can use these meetings to draw feedback and criticism out of people. If someone does step up to point out a problem or air a grievance, thank the person and point out to everyone else how helpful the comments are. Expressing gratitude when people are candid will encourage others to be candid as well.

There are two important points about SEAL Team debrief meetings that apply to all organizations. First, the SEALs provide a designated time for people to call out problems and get things off their chests, which removes many of the barriers to providing candor. Second, Matt's open response to the new guy's criticism encouraged others to be candid in the future. Organizations with cultures of candor are healthier than those without, and the best way to instill candor is to practice it and reward others for doing the same.

Along with candor, another method to combat the Avoidance Trap is to honor accountability. All of us make mistakes; to err is human. But in many cultures, particularly in larger organizations, flawless execution is honored above all else. Mistakes are frowned upon and seen as badges of shame. When someone messes up in this kind of environment, they try to keep it hidden. Human error is inevitable, so an organization whose culture relies upon flawless execution is inherently flawed—that's one of life's ironies. It takes courage to admit we've done something wrong, and the more painful that admission is to make at your organization, the less likely people are to do it. If we see others suffer painful consequences for admitting mistakes, we're going to hide our own. Conversely, when we see that those who own up to their mistakes are viewed in a positive light, we are more likely to do so ourselves. When mistakes are viewed as opportunities for learning and improvement, it is much easier for people to admit to them. The essence of accountability is not about punishing mistakes; it is about giving everyone the opportunity to succeed in a transparent way. So, how do you create a culture of accountability? Practice it and preach it.

The best way to instill accountability into a culture is to practice it. In the SEAL Team 6 story, Matt immediately owned up to his mistake of micromanaging the new guy, and he did so in front of the whole team. This sent a strong message. Matt's response is a great example of candor and accountability working together. The new guy candidly called out what he felt was Matt's mistake in leadership, and in response, Matt held himself accountable for his failure.

A more formal method of practicing accountability is to incorporate it into the regular flow of information. A great way to ensure members of a team stay current on what others are up to is implementing a weekly reporting requirement, such as a 3-and-3 report. Each team member commits to three goals he or she will accomplish in the coming week and reports on their performance against last week's commitments. Team members communicate these commitments both in writing and in-person at a weekly team meeting. Team members who fall short on a commitment have the opportunity to explain why they failed and what they're going to do about it. When this level of reporting happens consistently, people find it easy to hold themselves accountable without having to muster courage. Knowing they will need to account for their progress at next week's meeting keeps people focused on achieving their goals.

Preaching accountability also helps instill it into a culture. I don't mean preaching from a pulpit; I mean making accountability part of the language of your organization. Words matter and can go a long way to lay the foundation for a culture of accountability. Regular organizational mantras that honor accountability prepare people for the inevitability that they are going to make mistakes, and make it clear that the path to success is filled with trial and error. When people understand mistakes are necessary for growth, they will no longer fear failure.

Many successful cultures share quotations from famous people about mistakes and failure. This can be a great way to "preach" the message that failure is required for success. Here are a few quotations from some of the greats:

"I didn't fail the test; I just found 100 ways to do it wrong." – Benjamin Franklin

"Failure is simply the opportunity to begin again, this time more intelligently." – Henry Ford

"I've failed over and over and over again in my life. And that is why I succeed." – Michael Jordan

"It's fine to celebrate success but it is more important to heed the lessons of failure." – Bill Gates

When we understand that we must make mistakes in order to learn and grow, accountability becomes an honorable characteristic. And when we are confident that we are part of an organization that understands this, toxic fear of failure will not drive our behavior.

The bottom line is that we all make mistakes. One true test of character is how we react once we recognize we've made a mistake. Here's a story about a monster of a mistake.

PAMPERS GIFTS TO GROW

When I was on the executive team at ePrize, we were managing a loyalty program for Pampers diapers. The structure of the program was typical: buy diapers, get a code from the package, deposit it into your online account, earn points, and get cool stuff. Every package of diapers was printed with a unique fifteen-character alpha-numeric code, and our software team developed an algorithm to randomly generate millions of these codes.

There are only ten digits and only twenty-six letters in the alphabet, so when you randomly generate millions of fifteen-character alpha-numeric codes, you're going to get some real words popping up purely by chance. And sometimes they're nice words like:

GWZJQ27**LOVE**90H1

C0**CUTE**D5ORNLE59

MG9LJ3N87S**LOL**9B

But you can also get some not-so-nice words like:

5P**HATE**PQGQ4XZXL

KRF46TLEB1**DIE**72

Q6FSLHJ**KKK**7631C

It's a good idea to run these codes through a profanity filter before sending them to clients, ensuring nasty words aren't accidentally printed on, say, a package of diapers. And that's usually what we did. But, of course, mistakes are inevitable.

One day, Pampers asked for a new batch of codes, and someone from our company sent a list that hadn't been run through the profanity filter yet. Pampers printed those on hundreds of thousands of diaper packages. You might see where this is going....

Imagine the reaction of a young mother who had just bought a pack of diapers for her six-week-old daughter and was entering the code from the Pampers package into her loyalty account one Sunday morning in early spring.

If you've ever had the pleasure of holding a six-week-old baby, you know it's one of the purest experiences in the universe. That little, tiny human is just a bundle of love, joy, and innocence.

Well, this mother looked down at the package of Pampers in front of her and started entering in her code when she came across a four-letter word that virtually jumped off the packaging at her. And it wasn't one of the nice words. It was one of the bad ones...and I'm not talking about HATE or DIE. It was worse, *much* worse. In fact, this arguably is the worst four-letter word in the English language (and it did not start with "s" or "f").

As you can imagine, we received a call from Pampers. They were upset because they'd just gotten an angry call from that mother. In conflict-averse cultures, the instinctive reaction is to defend: *Our contract doesn't say anything about running codes through a profanity filter. You mean you have a profanity filter at Pampers, and you didn't run the codes through it before printing them on your packages, and now you want us to pay for it? Seems like you bear a great deal of responsibility here, but we're prepared to negotiate a resolution.*

But in a culture of candor and accountability, people don't launch into defensive postures in these situations. They step up, take responsibility for their mistakes, embrace the conflict, and view the incident as an opportunity to demonstrate the character of the organization. They say things like, "We are so sorry we put you in this terrible position with your customer. This is our mistake, and we're going to do whatever it takes to make this right."

Luckily, most of the packaging was still sitting on pallets in the warehouse, waiting to be shipped. So, we paid to break down and repackage everything, this time with codes that had gone through a profanity filter. We also reached out to the mother, explained the situation, apologized, and gave her a year's supply of Pampers on us.

The brand manager at Pampers was happy with our response. He said, "Wow, you really screwed that up. We've worked with other companies in the past who would have put up a fight. But you stepped up and took responsibility. We know that if we run into another problem, you've got our back and will protect our brand. We trust you to do the right thing."

The end result is that our relationship with Pampers was much stronger than it would have been had we executed flawlessly in the first place and never ran into conflict. It is true that quality execution is critically important to the success of any organization. But candor and accountability are just as critical, and sometimes even more so.

Since mistakes are inevitable, we might as well embrace the conflicts they cause. In fact, we should seek out conflicts as opportunities to demonstrate our character, build trust, and strengthen our relationships. In our organizations, we should celebrate examples of people taking accountability. This behavior is infectious; when others see it, they will copy it. Holding oneself accountable, especially when it hurts, is rare in our society and sets people apart. It doesn't take brains, exceptional talent, or an expensive education to accept responsibility for your errors. It simply takes integrity. While people might remember that you made a big mistake, they will certainly never forget that you stepped up and took responsibility. Adopting this perspective will prevent toxic fear from pulling you into the Avoidance Trap.

The SEAL Team 6 and Pampers stories are great examples of staying out of the Avoidance Trap. There are some very different lessons we can learn about the next conflict trap—the Judgment Trap—from a story on the other side of the world, which involves a Buddhist healing monk, a little girl named Ling, and a Chinese mafia boss.

UNDERSTANDING THE AVOIDANCE TRAP

Avoiding conflict makes it worse

In the short term, it may feel safer to avoid a conflict, but that allows the issue to fester and grow. Toxic fear causes us to run from conflict rather than embrace it for success. Most people will run away from a small conflict that is immediate, even if it sends us running toward a larger conflict that's not immediate.

Three sources of toxic fear that lead to the Avoidance Trap:

- **Lack of Psychological Safety:** Fear of being punished or humiliated for raising a concern or calling out a mistake.
- **Impression Management:** Fear that speaking up will put us in a negative light.
- **Socialization:** Fear that offering constructive criticism will come across as disrespectful, disagreeable, or impolite.

TOOLS TO OVERCOME THE AVOIDANCE TRAP

Make the initiation of conflict a job requirement
Regularly schedule debrief and pre-brief meetings in which people aren't doing their job if they remain silent. Benefits:

- Provide recurring opportunities to uncover problems, so that bad news surfaces faster.
- Create a psychologically safe environment that frees people from the social stigma of initiating conflict.
- Motivate and empower people to continually seek improvement.

It's a learning exercise, not an execution problem
Stress the importance of hearing everyone's unique perspective to get the broadest view possible.

Build a culture of candor and accountability
Encourage candid feedback, view mistakes as opportunities for learning and improvement (not badges of shame), and honor those who hold themselves accountable.

Make it a habit
Weekly reporting from each team member with commitments for the upcoming week and performance against last week's commitments.

Be a model
Regularly hold yourself accountable for your own mistakes.

Run toward conflict
Seek out conflicts as opportunities to demonstrate character, build trust, and strengthen relationships.

CHAPTER 5

The Judgment Trap

A BUDDHIST HEALING MONK, A LITTLE GIRL NAMED LING, AND A CHINESE MAFIA BOSS

Dr. Lu began his medical training at age three, when monks from the nearby Buddhist temple observed his extraordinary gift of insight. They knew that for Dr. Lu to achieve his maximum potential, he had to begin training immediately. So, with his parent's permission, they took him to live in the temple, where he remained well into adulthood. Dr. Lu trained all day, every day, as a healing monk. During that time, he also attended Western medical school and became an MD.

Several years ago, something happened to Dr. Lu that altered the course of his life, saved thousands of young children from a terrible fate, and revealed a lesson about the devastating power of judgment—and how to avoid it. And it involved a little girl named Ling.

Ling was born in Yan Qing, a poor farming community on the outskirts of Beijing, where most people live in poverty. Ling lived with her parents in her grandfather's house. When she was three years old, her mother abandoned the family.

Two years later, her father committed suicide. Ling's grandfather continued to care for her another six years until tragedy struck again and he was diagnosed with terminal cancer.

With just a few months left to live, Ling's grandfather had no one to call and no idea what to do. In a move of desperation, he sent word to Ling's mother that he was ill and could no longer care for her daughter. He didn't expect to hear back. After all, this woman had abandoned her daughter and husband. Miraculously, however, Ling's mother showed up and was reunited with her daughter. She said she had a good job in Beijing and could care for Ling, so she took her daughter to live in the city.

But it turned out there was no job. Ling's mother was a drug addict and prostitute, and as unthinkable as it is, she sold her daughter into sex slavery to feed her drug habit. Ling was eleven years old.

For the next two years, Ling was held captive and forced into prostitution. Her situation felt hopeless, and she doubted that she would ever know freedom again. Then one day, another prostitute noticed how young she was. She told her pimp (who only used adult prostitutes) about Ling's situation. The pimp got word to his boss's boss's boss: one of the four head mafia bosses who controlled all organized crime in Beijing.

This mafia boss happened to be a patient of Dr. Lu's, and he told the doctor about Ling. He gave Dr. Lu the address of where Ling was being held and promised that no one would give Dr. Lu or his people any trouble if they went to rescue her.

Dr. Lu gathered some friends and set out to find Ling. She was living in a tiny, dark, dirty, rat-infested apartment with seven other people. Dr. Lu told her he'd come to rescue her, and he convinced Ling to come with him and his friends. They quickly reached a safe location, but Ling was hysterical and traumatized. Dr. Lu asked the others to leave the room so he could try to calm her down. As he closed the door behind the last person and turned to face Ling—who was still sobbing—she started to take off her clothes.

"What are you doing?" he asked, his confusion giving way to the horror of what she might say.

"Isn't this what you want?" she said through her tears.

The full weight of Ling's tragic situation hit Dr. Lu, and he suddenly realized he couldn't continue living on this earth without doing something to help people like Ling. He managed to place her into a safe environment with a good family. Her new parents cared for her, gave her emotional support, homeschooled her, and slowly socialized Ling into an appropriate teenage life.

After rescuing Ling, Dr. Lu went back to his patient and convinced him to call a meeting with the four head bosses of the Beijing Crime Syndicate. Dr. Lu made lunch for them (he is an excellent cook), then made his "pitch" for why they shouldn't allow child prostitution in their organizations. He argued that even though some clients would pay more for child prostitutes, in the big picture it wasn't worth it. Ultimately, he persuaded the bosses to commit to not allowing their pimps to use children. They even developed a system to notify Dr. Lu's people whenever they learned of a child caught up in the sex trade.

Today, thanks to the efforts of Dr. Lu and the crime bosses, thousands of children have been kept off the path Ling was on. While there still is some child prostitution in Beijing, it has been dramatically reduced.

Dr. Lu went on to found an organization called Golden Courage International, which sponsors children from poverty to finish high school. Ling was among the first to be accepted into the program, and she was encouraged to put her past life behind her by giving herself a new name. She chose 新玲, which translates to New Hope. Today, Ling is a middle school geography teacher, and she's married with a daughter of her own. Ling has long since forgiven her mother and even tries to help her get clean in between jail stints.

Why have I told you this child prostitution story in a book on detoxing conflict? There is conflict everywhere you turn in this story: between mother and daughter, prostitute and pimp, Buddhist monk and mob boss, and more; and there are numerous points at which judgment could have easily pulled any of those people into the fourth Conflict Trap: the Judgement Trap. However, Ling and Dr. Lu were able to stay out of the trap, resulting in a new life for Ling that was unimaginable to her as a teenager, and also resulting in an organization that has altered thousands of lives for the better. Golden Courage International has a 100 percent success rate of kids not only graduating high school, but also going on to earn a college degree.

Many people would find it tremendously difficult to look past their negative judgments about someone like Ling's mother. But Ling learned to look beyond her own judgments and live a happy life. Meanwhile, many doctors in Beijing had serious reservations about treating crime bosses. Some were afraid for their own lives. Others felt it was morally wrong to provide medical service to individuals who were responsible for so much suffering. But Dr. Lu was not bound by the judgments that held other doctors back. He is able to see humanity in everyone, which paid off when he invited the four head mafia bosses to lunch and won their support. He avoided the Judgment Trap, which led to freedom for thousands of children like Ling.

We might not all be Buddhist healing monks, but we can all learn a few important things about overcoming judgment from this story.

HOW JUDGMENT HAPPENS

Our instinct to judge others has been honed by millions of years of evolution. Our prehistoric ancestors were under constant threat of attack from both wild animals and other humans who wanted to kill them or rob them of scarce resources. It has always been imperative for humans to quickly and accurately judge whether someone is a friend or foe. Studies show we make judgments within half a second of meeting a new person, and these judgments are more likely to be negative than positive. In the wild, the stakes are life and death, so it's best to err on the side of safety and assume everyone is an enemy until proven otherwise. That's why studies confirm humans learn negative judgments faster than positive ones—and negative judgments persist longer.

Judgment isn't a universally bad thing. Judgment is a natural and valuable tool that informs many of our decisions. We judge people and situations based on the information available to us, and these judgments are often helpful. Obvious examples include judging a dark alley in a rough neighborhood as unsafe; judging a nun volunteering at a homeless shelter as charitable; or judging a doctor with a degree from Harvard medical school to be a better surgeon than one with a degree from an online university you've never heard of.

Our judgments often save us from conflicts. For instance, if we know someone regularly leaks confidential information, we may judge him to be untrustworthy and decide not to share our secrets with him. If someone has a history of disputes with her business partners, we may judge her to be a liability and not worth doing business with. In these instances, judgment may be beneficial.

However, when judgment mixes with toxins like fear, anger, self-righteousness, or resentment, the resulting cocktail is a form of toxic judgment that can pull us into the Judgment Trap and spur negative conflict. While the types of threats we face in today's world have changed since we lived in caves, our instinctive, tribalistic judging processes have not. Threats to our survival have been replaced with threats to our job security, sense of acceptance, and self-confidence. With our ancient judging processes still firmly in place, we operate on fertile ground for toxic conflict. We are wired to judge and react to strangers, colleagues, friends, and family with fear, anger, and blame, like our ancestors did when it came to murderous tribes and saber-toothed tigers.

Sometimes our judgments close us off to possible solutions to our problems. For example, imagine you're lost but you won't ask a nearby person for directions at a gas station because he has a bumper sticker you find offensive. Or perhaps you ask for directions, but your judgment comes through in your tone and the person refuses to help you (or gives you directions to the wrong place). When toxic judgment stops us from working with others or interferes with our ability to communicate effectively, it can lead to conflict. This is the Judgment Trap.

Because we are tribal in nature, we're always looking to identify with one group and distinguish ourselves from another. This phenomenon, known in psychology as in-group/out-group bias, creates a tendency to build a framework in our minds that puts us higher up than others, and which leads to judgment and conflict. When a friend posts a political opinion on social media, we label and judge him for it (after all, *he clearly cares more about his political party than he does about the country*). When a coworker shows up to the office in sweatpants, we judge her (*have a little pride in your appearance, you slob*). When we allow these types of judgments to dominate our thought process, our brains use them as substitutes for unknown facts about others. We make assumptions. This leads to negative conflict because we don't know why our coworker showed up in sweatpants today. There may be a perfectly good explanation. When our judgments kick in, we might assume she's a slob who doesn't take work seriously before we have all the facts.

Our judgments inform how we communicate, and like the other Conflict Traps, there are two sides to the Judgment Trap: the person doing the judging, and the person being judged. Regardless of which side of toxic judgment someone is on, there are consequences that affect everyone involved.

THE CONSEQUENCES OF TOXIC JUDGMENT

There are three main responses to judgment that characterize it as toxic. If we feel judgment within ourselves or from others but we don't experience these consequences, the judgment is not toxic. However, when one or more of these consequences occur, we are in the Judgment Trap. The first consequence is when judgments prevent us from working with others in a productive way; the second is when they lead to judgmental communication that triggers negative responses from others; and the third is when our own judgments weigh us down, consuming valuable time and energy.

1. Prevents Us from Working with Others

The first negative result of toxic judgment is that it can keep us from collaborating with certain people or organizations, which can impede progress. Imagine if Dr. Lu had judged the mafia boss and refused to see him as a patient. Most people would support that decision. After all, he's a *criminal*. But if Dr. Lu had turned that patient away, thousands of children would have become caught up in the sex trade—clearly a bad outcome.

Imagine that two brilliant scientists are working on a promising cure for cancer when one of them learns that the other has been cheating on his wife. The former harbors such strong judgment toward his colleague's immoral behavior that he stops working with him. As a result, they do not cure cancer and millions continue to succumb to this deadly disease.

When our judgments cause us to do things that interfere with our goals, that's a trap. It's understandable that a scientist might have feelings about a colleague's infidelity. But if his goal is to cure cancer and the best chance of doing that is to work together, then allowing judgment to pull him away from that goal would be a trap; it prevents progress. This is the Judgment Trap, and it is not limited to individuals. It can work on a societal level too.

Research on one of the most promising therapeutics for a wide variety of illnesses and diseases was derailed in the United States for nearly fifty years because of toxic judgment. Back in the mid-twentieth century, lysergic acid diethylamide (LSD) and other psychedelic medications were the subject of serious medical research by leading academics at prestigious universities like Stanford and Harvard. In the 1950s and '60s, psychedelic medications were frequently referred to in both academic and popular writings as promising potential treatments for post-traumatic stress disorder (PTSD), drug and alcohol addiction, depression, anxiety, and more. But by the mid-sixties, the same substances were also entering popular culture as "mind-altering" drugs associated with hippies and a counterculture attitude.

LSD's hippie reputation caused both politicians and medical leaders to frown upon the substance. Members of the establishment did not like members of the anti-establishment and judged them negatively. Anything hippies were doing was negative by association: long hair, loud music, raggedy clothes, and drug use. The Controlled Substances Act, passed in 1970, included harsh penalties for the manufacture, possession, and use of many psychedelics. This limited further research; medicinal development ground to a halt.

To make matters worse, the CIA attempted to "weaponize" psychedelic drugs in the 1950s and '60s. Under the codename Project MK-Ultra, the CIA conducted a series of top-secret mind-control experiments that included secretly dosing American citizens with LSD without their knowledge. Let that sink in for a minute. Imagine how you would react if someone secretly slipped a dose of LSD into your morning coffee. That would freak the hell out of most people, which is exactly what happened in hospitals, universities, and prisons around the country.

In one of the more extreme scenarios—Operation Midnight Climax—the CIA paid prostitutes to lure unsuspecting "johns" to what looked like an ordinary hotel room, where the men were dosed with LSD while their actions were observed by CIA operatives from behind a two-way mirror—American tax dollars at work.[26] Despite the bad actors conducting unethical research (like the CIA), the field of psychedelic medicine still showed real promise and had the potential to benefit millions. An objective, dispassionate response would have been to regulate the research and punish the bad actors. There was nothing in the raw data coming out of the research to warrant absolute prohibition of all psychedelic substances, but that is what happened. The wholesale shutdown of research was an irrational political response fueled by toxic judgment that was not based in science. The judgments by those in power brought them in direct conflict with scientific and medical progress—and judgment won out.

---

26 Nofil, Brianna. "The CIA's Appalling Human Experiments With Mind Control." History.com. https://www.history.com/mkultra-operation-midnight-climax-cia-lsd-experiments. Accessed October 19, 2021.

Consequently, research and innovation were put on hold for nearly half a century.

Recently the negative stigma surrounding psychedelics has faded, and legitimate research has resumed. Patients with severe depression, anxiety, and PTSD have seen significant improvements from psychedelic medications in clinical settings.[27] A number of US cities—including Denver, Detroit, Oakland, Santa Cruz, and Ann Arbor—have decriminalized psychedelic plants and fungi, and more cities are following the trend, but it's a slow process.[28, 29, 30, 31] We still have over

27 Belouin, Sean J. and Henningfeld, Jack E. "Psychedelics: Where we are now, why we got here, what we must do." ScienceDirect.com. February 21, 2018. https://www.sciencedirect.com/science/article/pii/S0028390818300753 - bib45. Accessed October 19, 2021.

28 Way, Art. "Denver Makes History, Becomes First U.S. Jurisdiction to Decriminalize Psilocybin Mushrooms." DrugPolicy.org. May 8, 2019. https://drugpolicy.org/press-release/2019/05/denver-makes-history-becomes-first-us-jurisdiction-decriminalize-psilocybin. Accessed October 19, 2021.

29 Asmelash, Leah and Ahmed, Saeed. "Oakland residents won't be busted for using 'magic mushrooms' and other psychedelic drugs." CNN.com. June 5, 2019. https://www.cnn.com/2019/06/05/health/oakland-decriminalizes-magic-mushrooms-trnd/index.html. Accessed October 19, 2021.

30 Carpenter, David E. "Santa Cruz Is Third U.S. City To Decriminalize Psilocybin, Plant Medicine, As Advocacy Expands." *Forbes*. February 1, 2020. https://www.forbes.com/sites/davidcarpenter/2020/02/01/santa-cruz-is-third-us-city-to-decriminalize-psilocybin-plant-medicine-as-advocacy-expands/?sh=421e36a55d0d. Accessed October 19, 2021.

31 Stanton, Ryan. "Why Ann Arbor officials decided to decriminalize psychedelic mushrooms, plants." Mlive.com. September 22, 2020. https://www.mlive.com/news/ann-arbor/2020/09/why-ann-arbor-officials-decided-to-decriminalize-psychedelic-mushrooms-plants.html. Accessed October 19, 2021.

fifty years of judgment to overcome. This is an example of the Judgment Trap preventing people from working together at the societal level.

Whether we're talking about a doctor refusing to treat a mob boss, a scientist who won't collaborate with an adulterer, or an entire political establishment that discredits research on medicines associated with "hippies," judgment is toxic when it prevents us from working with others to achieve our goals. It acts as a barrier to collaboration that can hamper progress and stop us from reaching our collective potential. That's the first negative consequence of toxic judgment.

2. Communication that Triggers Negative Responses

The second problem with toxic judgment is that it comes across in communication, which creates and escalates conflict. When people speak to us in a judgmental tone or with judgmental language, we can become defensive, resentful, and angry.

Judgmental communication often comes across as condescending. Most of us resent being judged. This can cause us to dig in on our position and close ourselves off from considering the other side's perspective. Subconsciously, we feel that if we give in on an issue, it will validate the other person's negative judgment of us. If we acknowledge that a judgmental person is correct on a certain point, that would be an admission to them—and to ourselves—that their negative judgments were correct. That could validate the hierarchy in the other person's mind, confirming that he is superior to us. So we defend our position, not necessarily because we strongly believe in it, but because we feel we're defending something much more important: our position within the hierarchy—our sense of self.

Our judgments of others often affect them in the same way. Someone may lead a lifestyle or engage in behavior we do not approve of, and we judge them for it. Though we may not consciously acknowledge our judgments of others to ourselves, the judgments reside in our minds as feelings. Other times we are fully aware of our judgments and choose to hold tight to those strong opinions. If we hold a judgment about a person we never have to see again, it doesn't matter. But if we expect to interact with this person, clear communication is important. Left unchecked, judgment comes across in our words and tone of voice, which can create new conflict or fan the flames of an existing one.

We often perceive the judgments of others as indictments of our own character. Sometimes this is an overt thought; other times it is subconscious. Any time a person claims he's been wronged by another, it can be construed as an indictment of character.

- Someone claims you cut in line at the coffee shop (implying that you're a cheater).

- Your next-door neighbor complains you ran over his lawn when backing out of the driveway (implying you're careless).

- Someone accuses you of stealing her parking space (implying you're selfish).

When we're on the receiving end of these accusations, we feel judged. Perhaps the judgment is appropriate (maybe we were careless or did it on purpose). In those situations, most of us are inclined to accept the judgment and apologize. But when the judgment is unwarranted or the response is an over-reaction, our defense mechanisms prevent us from acknowledging our shortcomings. We start making our own negative judgments right back. That's when judgment reaches toxic levels, causing the conflict to escalate.

Toxic judgmental communication, whether intentional or unintentional, acts as a barrier to conflict resolution and fans the flames of conflict, pulling us into the Judgment Trap. In a moment we will discuss how to detox this negative judgment, but first there's one more negative consequence of toxic judgment to call out.

3. Consumes Time and Energy

The third consequence of toxic judgment is that it encourages us to hold on to toxins like fear and anger, which consume time and energy. We can waste years stewing over someone who wronged us instead of putting that energy to better use. One example comes from a friend of mine named Jennifer.

Jennifer's father left her mother for a much younger woman (who was only four years older than Jennifer herself). Understandably, Jennifer was angry at her father for hurting her mother and breaking up their family. She judged his behavior as wrong and felt he should be punished. This judgment justified her anger toward him because, after all, that's what he deserved.

Jennifer's judgment gave her anger purpose and made her feel dignified in holding a grudge. It became the defining characteristic of her relationship with her father, dominating every interaction with him and every conversation about him. Her judgment continually reinforced the idea that he was wrong and deserved the punishment she was doling out. Her anger consumed time and energy that would have been better spent pursuing Jennifer's own goals.

Jennifer later acknowledged that for years she felt weighed down and held back by her judgment. Despite the time and energy she spent judging her father, his behavior did not change. Her judgments didn't compensate for the wrongs perpetrated against her mother either. All the judgment did was consume a lot of Jennifer's time and energy.

We all go through life with the goal of ensuring our basic needs are met. These needs range from physical well-being (food, shelter, safety, and exercise), to connection (love, belonging, appreciation, and acceptance), to autonomy (freedom, space, independence, and choice), to meaning (purpose, growth, self-expression, and competence). When these needs are met, we feel content. When they're not met, we might feel scared, angry, or sad. We all have experienced this in one form or another, and we know how much energy it consumes. This emotional process leads straight into the Judgment Trap, and the longer we spend there the more damage our judgments inflict. Time and energy are limited resources, and the more we waste judging others the less we have available for achieving our goals. That's the third consequence of toxic judgment.

Toxic judgment separates us from our goals. Whether it prevents us from working with others, interferes with communication, or consumes time and energy, toxic judgment is bad. This is true at an individual level as well as on an organizational or societal scale. The good news is that there are some steps we can take to raise our awareness when it comes to judgments. These steps will keep judgment from interfering with our goals and empower us to communicate with others in ways that don't perpetuate toxic conflict.

HOW TO DETOX JUDGMENT

These three consequences of toxic judgment are pervasive, insidious, and completely avoidable. But with some simple strategies, we can steer clear of the Judgment Trap, freeing us to reach our goals and create more fulfilling relationships. I became aware of these tactics when I asked Dr. Lu how he was able to deal with the Beijing mafia bosses.

What was Dr. Lu's approach to staying judgment free with such reprehensible behavior happening in front of his eyes? He told me that, because of his training as a healer, he does not judge people. He sees people make decisions that hurt themselves and others, but he can't afford to judge them because he is focused on healing. He is often very blunt with people and will say things like, "The chemicals you're ingesting into your body are killing you. If you want to live you need to stop." or "The food you're giving your child is killing him. He won't die tomorrow, but you are taking years, even decades, off his life." And by the way, Dr. Lu says these things with a Shopping List Voice. His words are direct, but he delivers them without judgment.

Back to pimps and mafia bosses. "I don't see them as pimps," Dr. Lu told me. "I see them as people. I have no fear or anger toward the mob bosses. I'm simply sharing my perspective and asking them to share theirs with me. People are people; no one is truly better or worse than anyone else."

Of course, he's a Buddhist monk whose worldview is deeply rooted in a spiritual belief system. Dr. Lu has a leg up on most of us. I am not one to preach about the spiritual oneness of the universe. But I am focused on conflict and how to leverage it for good. We know that the vast majority of conflict can be improved with better communication. Judgments and preconceived notions interfere with our ability to communicate effectively. But we all have the power to set our judgments aside, or to at least consciously consider how our judgments impact our decisions and communication. This awareness is the key to detoxing judgment.

Ling is a perfect example of someone who has steered clear of the Judgment Trap. Despite the fact that her mother first abandoned her and later sold her into sex slavery, Ling does not hold any grudges or negative judgements and their relationship is conflict free. Most importantly, Ling is happy. Similarly, the mafia bosses had done plenty to warrant negative judgment, but Dr. Lu did not judge them, and many thousands of children were saved as a result.

It's natural for us to make judgments. Sometimes they can be helpful (like when they protect us from people who want to do us harm), but other times they separate us from our goals. Thankfully, we have the strength, through awareness, to put our judgements into perspective and not allow them to drive us into toxic conflict. Here's how:

Use Judgment from Others as an Opportunity to Learn

Judgment from others can be a healthy driver of positive behavior. None of us is immune to ever being wrong or behaving in ways we regret. In those scenarios, someone's judgment of us might be appropriate. Sometimes we need to feel judged to become aware of our shortcomings. It's never a fun moment, but it's valuable to anyone willing to grow from it.

I was once in a meeting with several colleagues when John, whom I didn't know well, suggested a course of action I disagreed with. I was immediately dismissive of John's suggestion. I did not notice that my reaction caused John to withdraw from the discussion for the rest of the meeting.

As we walked out afterward, I noticed Susan—whom I've known for many years and respect—shaking her head at me with a judgmental expression on her face. I had seen that expression before and knew what it meant. I shot her a return look, asking, *What did I do?* She glanced at John and then back at me with a look that said, *If you don't know what you did, then I'm even more ashamed of you.*

This wordless exchange took less than two seconds, but her judgment weighed on me like a lead blanket. I quickly realized I'd fallen into the Bully Trap with John and potentially set the Avoidance Trap for future group discussions. I apologized to John and we ended up having a good conversation that set a positive tone between us. I often think about that incident as a reminder of how subtly our behavior can impact others. It has raised my level of awareness.

When someone's judgment makes us aware of our misdeeds and causes us to take ownership of our behavior, that's healthy conflict. But if we allow our defense mechanisms to drive our reaction to someone's judgment of us, we miss out on an opportunity for personal growth. A natural defense mechanism to Susan's judgment could have been to protect myself from the shame of my mistake by justifying my dismissive attitude toward John. That would have established a negative rapport between us and likely would have created conflict in the future that consumed energy.

The benefit of my exchange with Susan was that I recognized her judgment of me for what it was: I'd made a mistake and she had judged me for it. Her judgment was appropriate. When I felt her judgment, I resisted the urge to rationalize my behavior and protect against the shame from Susan's eyes or the threat to my self-confidence. Instead, I recognized that she was giving me feedback I needed.

The next time you feel someone else's judgment, resist the natural inclination to defend yourself. Instead seek to understand *why* you are being judged. You may realize you've erred and can correct your behavior. For example, if you unknowingly cut in front of someone in line, you can apologize and give them their place back.

Sometimes you may realize that someone's judgment is more about *their issues*, rather than your behavior. For example, maybe a coworker is speaking to you in a condescending tone because they graduated from a more prestigious university than you. This has nothing to do with you. Don't let your coworker's tribal fixation on academic achievement trigger you into wasting energy thinking about their judgments.

Communicate Without Judgment

Your communication style can either spread toxic judgment, or detox it. We all have preconceived notions about others. Nonjudgmental communication is about making sure we don't express those judgments in ways that create conflict or separate us from our goals.

When someone triggers a judgment within us, we immediately find ourselves at a crossroad. Even if we ignore our judgments intellectually we will still feel them, and they will still come across in our communication. But if we admit to ourselves that the other person has triggered judgments within us, we are then in a position to consciously choose whether to make those judgements known or to communicate without judgment.

My friend Bruce shared a small story of a time when he arrived at this crossroad. For several years, Bruce's mother had an in-home caregiver, Anne. One day, Anne informed Bruce's family that she was switching companies. They liked Anne and wanted to continue working with her, so Bruce contacted the new company and made arrangements. A week later, Bruce received a letter from the owner of the old company. It claimed Bruce could not hire Anne through any other company and threatened legal action.

There aren't many things that escalate conflict faster than the threat of "legal action." When most people receive a threat like that, they feel heightened levels of fear and anger, just like our ancestors did when their survival was threatened. Unfortunately, these uncomfortable feelings tend to lead to negative judgments about the other person. We might assume they are mean, difficult, a bully, or stupid (or maybe even all of the above). Those judgments fuel our response.

Bruce is a former lawyer, and he recognized that there were no legitimate legal concerns in the letter. He judged the company owner negatively for taking such an aggressive approach. It was clearly not well thought out on her end. He made assumptions about her leadership style and started to wonder if her personality was what had motivated the caregiver to switch companies in the first place. An equally aggressive response began to take shape in his mind before he'd even finished reading the letter. He was ready to fight fire with fire by sending an aggressive letter right back.

But there was something else. Bruce had gotten to know the owner of the old company over the years and the letter seemed out of character for her. Even though he was annoyed and had started to form negative judgments about her, he put those judgments aside and focused on the inconsistency between his past experiences with the company owner and the letter he'd just received. Bruce stopped his fight-or-flight response from being triggered and was able to consider the possibility that there was more to the story.

Instead of firing off a letter and escalating the conflict, Bruce picked up the phone and gave her a call. None of his judgments were on his mind during their conversation. Instead, he was genuinely interested to hear what was going on. He approached the conversation with empathy and compassion. And as a result, the company owner opened up to him. She admitted she'd been hurt when the caregiver went to work for a competitor, and she was having trouble dealing with her anger. She said the letter had been written by a lawyer long ago for a different situation entirely and she'd just changed the date and sent it to Bruce. She acknowledged she'd taken this emotional step without considering how the letter reflected on her.

Bruce's negative judgments might have been justified, but acting upon them would have likely escalated the conflict and consumed a tremendous amount of time and energy. "Winning" the conflict would have been a far less valuable result than the one Bruce achieved through a phone call. When Bruce approached the conversation with genuine curiosity and compassion, he detoxed the judgmental tone from his communication. This is a good example of staying out of the Judgment Trap by communicating without judgment, even though judgment may have been warranted.

When we judge someone, we can use non-judgmental words to communicate without conveying our judgments to that individual. A useful tool that helps detox judgment from communication is to focus on describing rather than on evaluating. For example, instead of saying, "This room is a pigsty; it is the messiest thing I have seen," a parent could say, "There are clothes on the floor and a banana peel on the desk that need to be picked up." The word "pigsty" may not have any judgment associated with it when describing a location on a pig farm, but it sounds very judgmental when describing someone's bedroom. By choosing not to use that word, the parent can cleanse toxic judgment from their communication. This parent may be fighting this messy room battle for quite some time, but at least the child is unlikely to be triggered into a defensive reaction.

If you find yourself in a disagreement, you can limit judgmental communication by focusing on the legitimacy of the other person's claim, rather than on your opinion of the person. Resist the urge to reach a conclusion before hearing them out. Tap into your genuine curiosity to get a better understanding of the person's position and let that drive your communication. Ask for solutions, and if she suggests one, ask her to walk you through how it will achieve the desired goal. This approach shifts your focus away from concluding the other person is wrong and instead toward the possibility that she may have a valid point. It also causes you to adopt a non-judgmental tone and choose non-judgmental words without having to actively think about it. The discussion will naturally focus on the best resolution to the disagreement.

Sometimes, allowing judgment to come across in our communication can be very helpful. The key is that the communication of judgment be a conscious decision, not a thoughtless, emotional reaction. In my example with Susan and John from above, I behaved in a way that triggered judgment in Susan, and she responded by giving me an unmistakably judgmental look. This was intentional on Susan's part. She knew me well enough to understand that communicating her judgment to me was the most efficient way to provide the feedback I needed at that moment. Susan didn't fall into the Judgment Trap because she was conscious of her judgment and deliberate in her communication of it.

Use It, Then Lose It

Hold onto a judgment as long as it's useful, then let it go when it's not. Energy is a limited resource. The more we judge others, the less energy we'll have left over for achieving our own goals. But we always have the ability to opt out and let go.

When someone hurts us or does something we don't like, we naturally judge them for it. If we use the lessons from that judgment to inform our decisions, then it's actually a good thing. For instance, when someone leaks information we shared in confidence, we might judge them to be untrustworthy and decide not to share confidential information with that individual again. That's a smart way to protect ourselves from potential harm. But that's where we need to drop it. If we allow our judgment to consume additional time and energy by assigning blame and doling out punishment (badmouthing him to our coworkers and excluding him from important meetings), we are putting energy into something that doesn't advance our goals.

Ling forgave her mother despite the terrible things she did. Ling certainly judges her mother as morally compromised and untrustworthy. And this judgment is valuable because it prevents her from putting herself in a position where she can be hurt by her mother again. This is healthy judgment because it helps Ling make good decisions about her safety without consuming much energy.

Many people feel Ling's mother behaved terribly and deserves Ling's judgment (along with a healthy dose of punishment and scorn). That might be true, but it's also irrelevant as far as Ling's happiness and goals are concerned. Ling understands that continuing to feel fear and anger toward her mother would fuel toxic judgment and only lead to more conflict. Ling accepts the limitations of her mother's ability to develop unconditionally loving relationships with people, a skill that is covered in more detail in Chapter 7, Don't Get Mad at Penguins Because They Can't Fly. Ling has decided she finds value in maintaining a relationship with her mother, which is her right. She does not put energy into judging, blaming, or punishing her mother and has not done so for a long time. The result is that she has stayed out of the Judgment Trap. Healthy judgment acts not as a roadblock, but rather as a guardrail, setting the boundaries of the relationship so that it remains valuable to Ling.

It's natural to want to assign blame and dole out punishment to those who hurt us, but it's far more valuable to recognize that when we externalize our feelings and jump to assign blame, we give control of our own happiness to someone else. If Ling had spent more energy judging her mother, she would have had less capacity to become a teacher, get married, and be a loving mother to her own daughter—all of which are more important to her than judging her mother. If she allowed toxic judgment to distract her from those wonderful things in her life, Ling would have fallen into the Judgment Trap.

Harboring judgment, assigning blame, and doling out punishment take energy away from pursuing our goals. Others may deserve our judgment, but we don't deserve the burden of carrying it. Judgment fuels toxins like fear and anger that hurt us. The extent to which we allow our time and energy to be consumed by toxic judgment is also the extent to which we fall victim to the Judgment Trap.

Whenever you feel your judgment has been triggered and you realize you've become focused on assigning blame and doling out punishment, hit the pause button. Recognize that your judgment has been triggered and shift your focus inward. It is highly unlikely that you will be in a situation that warrants the same levels of fear, anger, and blame our ancestors felt when a hostile tribe sought to steal their winter food stores. So instead, use your judgments to help you progress toward your goals, then let them go once they no longer serve you.

Conscious awareness of your judgment gives you power. When you notice yourself slipping into the Judgment Trap, recognize that you are voluntarily giving someone else power over your feelings. You are allowing judgment to consume time and energy you could be devoting to your own needs. Whether your coworker betrayed your confidence, your in-law spoke to you in a judgmental tone, or your mom sold you into prostitution, hold onto your judgment just long enough to be useful, then drop it. We all have the strength to keep toxic judgment in check and stop ourselves from falling into the Judgment Trap. If Ling can do it, so can we.

Next, we're going to look at another way in which communication plays a critical role in conflict. You'll learn how to remove toxic emotions from an interaction by making the other person feel like you understand their feelings. We'll visit the middle school math student who didn't follow the order of operations, the surgeon who cuts into a patient before diagnosing a medical condition, and the plumber who starts digging up a pipe before understanding where the leak is....

UNDERSTANDING THE JUDGMENT TRAP

Not all judgment leads to a trap

Judgment can be a valuable tool that informs our decisions. But when judgment mixes with toxins like fear, anger, self-righteousness, or resentment, the resulting cocktail is a form of toxic judgment that distracts us from our goals and creates unhealthy conflict.

Judging is a natural impulse

Our judgmental instincts were lifesaving for our ancestors, who had to make quick decisions based on very little information. Today we no longer face life-or-death situations, but our brains are still wired to react like our ancestors' did in response to saber-toothed tigers.

The consequences of toxic judgment

- **Prevents us from working with others:** When our judgments stop us from working with someone, even though that person can serve our larger objective, the Judgment Trap has prevented us from accomplishing our goals.
- **Communication triggers negative responses:** Our judgment of someone can come across in our tone of voice and choice of words, causing them to get defensive, resentful, and angry.
- **Consumes time and energy:** Even if someone is deserving of our judgment, holding onto judgment weighs us down and consumes valuable time and energy that could be going towards achieving our goals.

TOOLS TO OVERCOME THE JUDGMENT TRAP

Use judgment from others as an opportunity to learn
Being judged never feels good, but sometimes we need to feel judged in order to recognize our shortcomings so that we can improve.

Communicate without judgment
Focus on describing rather than evaluating. It is possible for us to feel judgment and still choose non-judgmental words.

Use it then lose it
Judgment is useful if it protects us from harm or progresses us towards our larger goal, but as soon as our judgment stops doing those things, it is more productive to let it go.

CHAPTER 6

Making People Feel Heard

*You might be hearing me, but
you're not listening to me.*

– A frustrated person
engaged in toxic conflict

One of the biggest challenges of communication is that when others speak, we often hear what we want to hear rather than what they actually are saying. This leads to misunderstandings, hurt feelings, and failed attempts to connect.

The single greatest source of toxic conflict is poor communication. Bad listening is usually at the heart of most unresolved arguments and heated disagreements. The best antidote to this toxin is to master the art of making others feel we genuinely understand them.

GENUINE LISTENING IS HARD

In order to make people feel heard, we must first listen to them. It may sound obvious, but careful listening is a critical skill for resolving conflict. In fact, most conflicts cannot be resolved unless one person carefully listens to and understands the other, and then communicates that understanding. The goal of this chapter is to empower you to be that person.

Listening to others becomes difficult in situations involving emotionally charged issues or entrenched beliefs. One reason for this is a well-studied psychological phenomenon: confirmation bias. This refers to the human tendency to favor information that confirms our existing beliefs and to ignore information that contradicts those beliefs. We tend to see what we are looking for rather than what is actually there. When speaking to someone who holds a belief opposite to our own, instead of seeking to understand the basis for her arguments, we often search for faults in her statements as confirmation that we are right and she is wrong.

Warren Buffett, one of the most successful investors ever, summed up confirmation bias perfectly when he said, "What the human being is best at doing is interpreting all new information so that their prior conclusions remain intact." Confirmation bias explains why it's virtually impossible to convince a staunch Democrat or Republican to acknowledge that their candidate might have serious flaws.

I had an eye-opening lesson about the power of confirmation bias in a negotiations seminar I took in law school. As class began, the professor strolled into the room empty-handed. This was noteworthy because he usually entered juggling a briefcase, our required reading, and sometimes a written exercise or two.

"Raise your hand if you're pro-life?" he asked, jumping right in without any chit-chat. I immediately thought, *Whoa, he's gonna go there. This will be interesting.* I was surprised to see the class was split pretty much down the middle (as it turns out, so is the country according to most polls). Then he paired up each pro-lifer with a pro-choicer and said,

> "Okay, this is a simple exercise. State your position to your partner and explain it. Second partner, all you have to do is repeat back the reasoning for your partner's position. The only rule is you cannot simply repeat back the exact words your partner said to you. You must restate your partner's reasoning in your own words."

What happened next was surprising, funny, and profoundly insightful into the dynamics of human communication. Most people could not do it. I heard many conversations around me in which students felt unheard by their partners:

Student 1: "I'm pro-choice because I don't believe the government has the right to tell a woman what to do with her body."

Student 2: "Understood. So, you believe it's more important for a woman to be able to avoid a medical inconvenience than it is to protect a human life."

Student 1: "That is NOT what I said."

Student 2: "Of course it is."

Student 1: "How dare you suggest that carrying an unwanted pregnancy to term, especially in the case of rape, is simply a 'medical inconvenience'!"

***

Student 3: "I'm pro-life because I believe an unborn child has the same right to life as any human who has already been born."

Student 4: "You're pro-life because you believe a bunch of men in Congress are in a better position to make medical decisions about a woman's healthcare than the woman herself."

Student 3: "What? I didn't say anything about medical decisions. I'm talking about protecting a human life."

***

Student 5: "I'm pro-choice because making abortion illegal won't stop abortions from happening; it will only stop them from being safe."

Student 6: "You want to make it easier and safer for a woman to kill her unborn child, rather than deal with the consequences of her behavior."

Student 5: "Were you even listening to me?"

I had gone through a couple years of law school with many of these students and knew they were reasonable, rational thinkers. It was surprising to watch them twist the words of their partners so quickly and severely. I struggled just as much as anyone that day to restate my own partner's arguments, so it was eye-opening on many levels.

Abortion is a perfect topic for this exercise because it is emotionally charged. People feel strongly about it. And many have strong feelings about the opposite position as well. People are very quick to take someone's position on abortion and extrapolate an entire set of beliefs and character judgments about them. That's why this topic is great here, because it taps into a pre-existing dialogue between people who have fundamentally different viewpoints.

Most difficult negotiations involve topics that are important to both sides. We become frustrated when our position falls on deaf ears, or when the other party refuses to acknowledge our point. In fact, it's infuriating. When others aren't willing to understand our position, we are less inclined to understand theirs. This creates a negative feedback loop.

Think about a scenario in which someone named Paul is trying to resolve a conflict with someone else. Paul puts his energy into explaining his position until he believes the other person gets it. He feels he cannot move to the next step toward resolution until this step is completed. That's because Paul will not want a resolution that doesn't take his position into account. The unspoken (and perhaps subconscious) thought is, *how can we reach a fair resolution without the other side knowing what my needs are and why I have those needs?* It would be very difficult to resolve the conflict without completing this step. And the longer that takes, the more energy Paul will spend and the more frustrated he will feel. As frustration builds, trust erodes, creating an ever-increasing hurdle that must eventually be overcome in order to reach a resolution. This hurdle not only makes the problem harder to solve, it also leaves the parties with less energy to solve it.

Now imagine you're on the other side of this conflict. Think about the collective benefit to both of you if you focus on this step Paul needs to move past and put your own energy into helping him move past it. The sooner you convince him you understand his position, the sooner you can work together to resolve the conflict, and the more energy you'll have between you to do it. Once you demonstrate your understanding of his position, Paul will feel heard and validated. Of course, it is equally important that he fully understands your position, and once he believes you understand him, he will be more motivated to understand you. All the energy you spared him by avoiding frustration can now instead be used to find a resolution.

At some point before you reached ninth grade, you probably learned about the mathematical order of operations. These are rules that govern the sequence in which multiple operations within a mathematical expression should be performed. I initially chose the legal profession because I'm bad at math, so this isn't going to be much of a refresher, but an example is that multiplication comes before subtraction, and items inside of parentheses take precedence over those outside the parentheses. If you go out of order and solve the addition before the division, you'll get the wrong answer. The same concept applies to a surgeon who begins operating on a patient before looking at an X-ray; or a plumber who starts digging up a pipe before understanding where the leak is coming from (incidentally, being bad at surgery and plumbing are two other reasons I chose the legal profession).

The same is true when resolving a conflict: if you try to negotiate a resolution before you understand the other side's position, you will get the wrong answer. Listen to the other person's position first so you can fully understand it. This step always comes before trying to resolve the conflict. However, even when we do this step in its proper sequence, confirmation bias often gets in the way of genuine listening, so we need to get over that hurdle first.

OVERCOMING CONFIRMATION BIAS

There are two things we can do to combat confirmation bias. The first is to be aware of how this tendency can cloud our judgment (easier said than done). The second is to specifically look for information that disproves our current beliefs. By forcing ourselves to examine the other side of the issue, we make sure we'll give it a fair and balanced evaluation.

There's a trick I came up with, back when I was a litigator, to remind myself of the power of confirmation bias. I always had a passion for my cases, which energized me to overcome any challenge that got in my way. This was generally good because if I didn't passionately believe in a case, I'd never be able to convince a judge or jury to believe either. However, this passion was also dangerous because it built a strong foundation for confirmation bias. The trick I learned was that if I ever felt like I couldn't lose a case, it was a warning sign that confirmation bias was clouding my judgment. I would get scared because that meant there was a threat I could not see. I wanted to fully understand all the ways I could lose so that

I could try to defend against them. Losing is bad enough, but getting blindsided by a threat I had failed to see is far worse.

This approach is useful in all types of conflicts, from business negotiations to personal discussions with family and friends. A great way to combat confirmation bias is to adopt the mindset that your position on any issue has flaws you aren't aware of, and that the opposite position has strengths that you do not yet see.

Vanity can also motivate you to combat confirmation bias: if you don't want to sound foolish or to appear closed-minded, know that confirmation bias will do both of those things. By assuming your knowledge is incomplete and your views are only partially formed, you'll train yourself to approach conflict-laden discussions with curiosity. Once you have adopted the mindset that there are surely weaknesses in your current thinking, the second thing you can do to combat confirmation bias is learn more about the opposing viewpoint.

The key is to aggressively seek out information that disagrees with your existing beliefs. Look for any information that will help uncover the flaws in your position. If you're engaged in a conflict with someone who has the opposite position, view that person as a source of information who can help you discover what you are missing. At this point, you are not trying to disprove the opposing viewpoint; you are simply trying to understand it. This approach has the added benefit of driving behavior that works toward conflict resolution. If you ask the other person questions from a place of genuine curiosity, that person is likely to perceive you as open-minded, and also as someone who desires to understand their position better.

The problem my professor highlighted during the abortion exercise isn't just a lawyer problem or a negotiation problem; it's a human problem. In conflict situations, most people don't listen to the other side's position, at least not genuinely. Rather, we tend to focus on the details that confirm our position and ignore those that contradict it. Then we start to internally plan our own response before the other person even finishes talking. Sometimes (probably more often than we'd like to admit), we make assumptions about their viewpoints and even about their overall character based on a few limited statements. But if we combat these natural tendencies of confirmation bias, we can flip the script.

Genuine curiosity promotes genuine listening. Genuine listening promotes genuine understanding.

Once you've overcome confirmation bias and you fully understand the other person's position, the next step is to communicate your understanding and make the other person feel heard. If you try to resolve the conflict before making the other person feel heard, you're messing up the order of operations and the entire process won't work. One common area where many people get the order of operations wrong is with apologies.

APOLOGIES

Apologies are a great example of how easily a lack of understanding can turn a conflict toxic. When someone delivers an apology that doesn't convey an understanding of why the other person is upset, the apology is as ineffective as the student who doesn't follow the order of operations in a math problem. These apologies generally don't work because they don't make the individual feel heard. Have you ever received an apology like this?

- "I'm deeply sorry if you are mad."

- "Sorry for whatever I did wrong."

- "If I hurt you in any way I am so, so sorry."

- "I apologize if I've somehow offended you."

Yes, these apologies incorporate phrases like "deeply sorry" and "so, so sorry," but they can feel hollow and insincere because they don't convey any understanding of why the person is upset. Further, there isn't an attempt to learn what the apology is for.

Apologies are about accountability. They should demonstrate an understanding of the consequences of our actions and a willingness to accept responsibility. Without those things, you don't have much of an apology. There are certainly instances in which people genuinely *feel* sorry but don't fully understand why. In this case, you can still apologize in a way that demonstrates a desire to be held accountable, and you can show that you feel sorry for not understanding what you did wrong: "I don't know what I did, but I see that I've upset you and I feel bad about that. I feel even worse that I don't know what I did. I may not deserve an explanation, but can you help me understand?"

In this example, you are expressing regret for having done some unknown action that hurt the other person, and regret for not understanding what you did wrong. And you are seeking to understand your error so you can take responsibility for making it right.

Being misunderstood can feel like an injustice. It's frustrating to receive shallow apologies. It can even feel like the other person is blaming you for feeling offended in the first place: *I know I didn't do anything to offend you, and it is unfortunate that you've chosen to react this way.* Apologizing for "whatever I did," doesn't demonstrate accountability or provide a sense of closure. Actually, it leaves the other party feeling offended and frustrated.

Before you can take any other steps to resolve a conflict, you first need to make the other person feel heard. You cannot make genuine progress until this is done.

IMPROVE THEIR ARGUMENT

One of the best strategies for making other people feel heard is to state their position better than they've said it themselves. Have you ever had the experience of fumbling with your words, trying to explain a difficult concept, when the person you were speaking with summed up your point in a single, concise sentence? It's a refreshing feeling of, *Oh, thank goodness, this person gets me!* Providing this same experience for others during a conflict will bring us closer to a swift and favorable resolution.

I first learned this principle in the courtroom. Losing in court doesn't feel good. And it's especially frustrating when the judge cuts you off and makes a ruling without letting you state your case. I remember judges cutting me off and saying things like. "Ok, I've got it," or, "Thanks. That's all I need." And I would be left biting my tongue, wishing I could finish explaining my position. I saw it happening to other lawyers, too, so I knew I wasn't alone in my struggle.

The reasons for this problem suddenly became clear after my first appearance in Judge Michael Talbot's courtroom. He ruled against me that day, but I left his courtroom confident that he'd heard me and understood my arguments. Judge Talbot was short tempered and often abusive to the lawyers who appeared before him, but I respected him as a judge because, while I didn't always like or agree with his rulings, I always felt he fully understood my position before making a decision.

One particular case was complicated, with multiple parties all represented by multiple lawyers (eight in total). We were about a year into the case, and there were several different issues we needed Judge Talbot to rule on. Each issue was supported by written motions, legal briefs, lengthy deposition transcripts, documents, and other evidence. It was a lot of paper. Normally, all of these documents are filed with the court in advance so the judge can read them all before the hearing. However, sometimes judges don't actually review everything prior to the hearing, and most judges listen to the attorneys argue their positions in the courtroom before deciding the case. This was a complicated case, and I expected there would be a lot of back-and-forth between the lawyers during the hearing.

But I was wrong.

"Wow, eight lawyers?" Judge Talbot asked with a good-natured chuckle as we made our way to the front of the courtroom. "Looks like you guys are paying for your kids' entire college education with the fees in this case." Everyone cracked up and the ice was instantly broken.

Then he made direct eye contact with me and held up a stack of documents covered in highlighter marks and post-it notes. "Karp, I've gone through everything you've submitted on this matter, so let me make sure I understand where you're coming from."

He proceeded to explain my own case exactly as I'd laid it out in my briefs. In fact, his summary hit every point I'd planned to cover in my presentation. He then moved on to each of the other attorneys, summarizing their arguments and hitting the important points. He articulated some of our arguments even better than we had in our briefs. He even said to one lawyer, "I noticed you didn't mention the evidence Karp cited in his brief; I assume you left that out because you think this evidence doesn't help your case. But if you want to correct me on that, go right ahead."

This guy had done his homework. He clearly articulated everyone's positions and he genuinely asked each of us to confirm that he'd gotten it right. He then issued his rulings and explained how he had arrived at his decisions. He homed in on a weakness in one of my positions and ruled against me (ouch). He clearly knew the case on a very deep level and had a firm grasp of every issue. I lost, but it didn't sting as much as usual.

Inspired by my experience that day with Judge Talbot, I now rely on the method he used any time I want someone else to hear what I'm saying, to agree with my position, or to follow my advice. The method is simple: before I explain my position to people, I first explain their position to them better than they said it themselves. Then I ask whether I've correctly understood their position or if I missed anything. If I'm genuinely interested in fully understanding their position, that sincerity will come across and help establish trust. Only after someone tells me there is nothing they'd like to add will I begin to explain my own point of view. In my experience, this approach brings clarity to the conflict sooner; oftentimes reveals that there is actually less in conflict between the two sides than originally thought; and quickly moves the focus toward resolving the points of contention. The earlier in a conflict you can achieve this clarity, the more energy both sides will have to spend on a fair resolution.

Whenever you are confronted with an opposing viewpoint or someone whose goals are in conflict with yours, focus on her position before discussing your own. Try to articulate her position more clearly than she did. If you are successful, she will immediately stop trying to explain her viewpoint, and the foundational step toward resolution will be complete. If you want someone else to agree with your views, you will find it requires significantly less effort once she is confident you've heard and understood her position first.

What I love about trying to improve the other person's argument is that it automatically puts you in a more attentive mindset. Instead of judging their ideas and planning your responses, you'll be working hard to understand and ask relevant questions because you'll know you're going to need to repeat everything in an even more convincing way. So your inner critic still gets to come out, but instead of looking for how wrong the other person's argument is, you'll be looking for ways to make it better.

As long as the other person doesn't feel heard and understood, it is extremely difficult to resolve a conflict. Feeling heard is a prerequisite for agreement and resolution.

EMOTIONS OVER LOGIC

The most powerful way to make people feel heard is to resonate with them emotionally. Feelings like frustration, anger, and fear become toxic when they are elevated to unhealthy levels. But when you can make someone feel heard, you'll be able to defuse these emotions and detox the conflict. One of the simplest ways to show someone you hear and understand them is by labeling their emotions.

In his bestselling book *Never Split the Difference*, former FBI hostage negotiator Chris Voss explains that labelling an emotion defuses the emotion. He says one of the keys to calming down terrorists and psychopaths at their wits' end is a technique he first mastered while working at a suicide hotline: labeling people's feelings.

Does the person you're talking to seem frustrated? Say, "Wow, that sounds really frustrating." Are they disappointed? Try, "I bet that was really disappointing for you." Or if you're in a conflict with someone who is depressed, you might say, "Hey, you seem really down about this."

When you put a specific name to the feeling you observe another person experiencing, you are labeling emotions. The beauty is that it doesn't matter if you're wrong about the emotion. In that case, the person will simply correct you. "No, I'm not frustrated," someone might say, "I'm just really tired right now." This gives you a better idea of what they are feeling and makes them feel heard.

An extremely effective way to show people you understand how they feel is to tell a story about a time when you felt the same. A great example comes from Danny DeVito's character in an episode of the Emmy-winning 1978 TV sitcom *Taxi*.[32] The show revolves around a group of cab drivers in New York City.

In this particular episode, DeVito's character, Louie de Palma, was caught spying on Elaine, another character, while she was changing clothes in the bathroom. She was furious at Louie and felt embarrassed and humiliated. Louie kept apologizing, but Elaine didn't believe him. She said he wasn't truly sorry because he didn't even understand what was wrong with what he did; he didn't have any idea how violated she felt.

That's when Louie opened up and told her a story. Danny DeVito, who plays Louie, is 4' 10" and has a very stocky build. He told Elaine how, twice a year, he has to go through the humiliating experience of shopping for clothes. He explained that the only way he can find anything that fits is to go to the boy's section and ask if they have any "husky" sizes. He said the worst moment is when he has to walk out of the dressing

---

32 *Taxi*. 1981. Season 4, episode 10, "Louie Goes Too Far." Directed by Michael Lessac, aired December 17, 1981 on ABC.

room in the new clothes and all the parents tell their kids not to stare. "Is that the way I made you feel when I peeked at you?" he asked.

"Kind of," she answered.

Then he teared up and said, "God, I'm sorry."

His story wasn't specifically about being spied on while changing clothes, but it showed that De Palma knew what Elaine was feeling on a deeply personal level. Once he did that, she was convinced that he knew exactly why his actions were wrong and understood the extent to which he'd hurt her. She realized his apology was genuine, and their conflict was resolved.

Making people feel heard is a critically important step in detoxing conflict. Next, let's talk about what to do when you've tried all of the other tactics in this book and nothing is working to solve a particularly grueling conflict. It's time to reveal how to stop getting mad at penguins.

UNDERSTANDING THE IMPORTANCE AND DIFFICULTY OF MAKING OTHERS FEEL HEARD

Making people feel heard is a critical step in resolving conflict

Most people will not be willing to consider other perspectives until they feel their perspective is fully understood. We can move conflicts toward resolution by understanding others.

Confirmation bias is a significant obstacle

Our emotional attachments to our pre-existing beliefs make our arguments weaker, not stronger. Only after we learn the strengths of other opinions and the weaknesses of our own ideas are we equipped to convince others we understand them so that we can resolve a conflict.

Genuine curiosity promotes genuine listening, and genuine listening promotes genuine understanding.

TOOLS FOR OVERCOMING CONFIRMATION BIAS AND MAKING OTHERS FEEL HEARD

Acknowledge confirmation bias has power
When we are consciously aware of confirmation bias, we have more control over our reactions.

Seek information that disproves your position
View the other person as a valuable resource to learn about the strengths and weaknesses in your position.

State the other person's position better than they said it themselves
When someone articulates your position better than you can, you feel understood. The sooner you can do that for someone else, the more motivated they will be to understand your position and work toward a resolution, and the more energy you'll have between you to do it.

Relate your understanding on an emotional level
Share a story of a time when you felt how the other person feels now, to demonstrate genuine understanding.

ORDER OF OPERATIONS FOR CONFLICT RESOLUTION

1) Understand the conflict by listening. Overcome confirmation bias by:
   a) acknowledging its power, and
   b) seeking out information that disproves previous way of thinking.

2) Communicate your understanding of the other side's position so they feel heard:
   a) state their position better than they said it themselves, and
   b) relate your understanding on an emotional level.

3) Work on a resolution.

CHAPTER 7

Don't Get Mad at Penguins Because They Can't Fly

Between expectation and reality is a space filled with suffering and conflict. The wider that space becomes, the greater our suffering is.

—Someone trying to sound like a wise old sage

Sometimes we can significantly reduce conflict and strife by simply accepting people as they are, limitations and all. When we stop expecting others to miraculously change into more caring, considerate, responsible, or [fill in the blank with whatever you want] people overnight, we can save ourselves much unnecessary hand-wringing. The phrase I often use to describe this is, *Don't get mad at penguins because they can't fly.* To explain, here is a quick story about my friend Dan and his business partner, James.

Dan and James built a company together and have been successful for many years. They make a great team and probably spend more time with each other than either of them spends with anyone else. One day, though, Dan confided in me that James reacts negatively whenever Dan achieves a big personal success. When Dan got engaged to his wife, for instance, James was annoyed. When Dan won a golf tournament, James was grumpy. When Dan was honored for charity work in the community, James was cold. And really anytime Dan is happy or proud about something, James becomes distant.

Dan took these reactions personally, and his frustration, anger, and resentment grew for years, compounding every time it happened. He tried to talk to James about it once, but James denied it and said Dan was imagining things. That just made Dan more frustrated. It was an ongoing conflict, and Dan didn't know what to do.

I'd gotten to know James well over the years, and I can confidently say he's an unhappy person. I don't know if it's genetic or the result of life experience—I just know he is not wired for happiness. It is sad to say, but even though James is undoubtedly funny, smart, and compassionate, happiness is beyond his ability.

Dan believes James is capable of being happy for Dan but chooses not to be, which naturally makes Dan mad. Whenever Dan shares good news, he secretly hopes James will be excited for him this time. But he's always disappointed.

When Dan shared all of this with me, I told him to "stop getting mad at penguins because they can't fly." What's this got to do with penguins? Here's what I said to Dan:

> "You keep waiting for James to be happy for you, and
> you get mad every time he's not. That's like getting mad
> at a penguin because it can't fly. 'What do you mean
> a penguin can't fly?' You might ask. 'It's a bird, it has

wings and feathers, and birds with wings and feathers can fly.' Except penguins can't. Flight is simply beyond their ability. Same thing with James. For some reason, it is beyond his ability to feel happiness for himself, let alone for you. The next time he gets annoyed when you have some good news to share, don't get mad at him and don't take it personally. It's not his fault that he is not capable of being happy for you. It's simply beyond his ability. Getting mad at him for that is like getting mad at a penguin because it can't fly."

Dan told me the situation happened again the very next day. Except this time Dan had accepted the reality that James has personal issues preventing him from feeling happiness for anyone else—that James was a penguin who couldn't fly. So, when James got annoyed over Dan sharing good news, Dan didn't take it personally because he expected that reaction. Instead, he thought, *this is simply James being James.*

Ever since adopting this perspective, Dan's frustration and anger have disappeared. He accepts James for who he is, limitations and all. He feels bad for James and wishes he could help him find happiness, but he now understands that is never going to happen. In recognizing that James is a penguin, Dan prevented his frustration from reaching toxic levels. He detoxed the conflict, and today his relationship with James is much healthier.

REMEMBER MILTON?

The idea of getting mad at penguins relates back to Milton from Chapter 3, The Need-to-Win Trap. Milton was the guy who needed to win. All. The. Time. As my client put it, *litigation is Milton's golf.* Lawsuits are sport to him. Milton wasn't capable of working toward a mutually agreeable resolution, or at least, it was against his nature. The thing that drove Milton, that gave him purpose in life, was a burning desire to fight and win. Milton was a penguin. This is a good time to revisit some of the Need-To-Win Trap lessons on how to deal with the Miltons of the world.

Remember, conflict swirls around Miltons like bees around honey, and dealing with a Milton can be exhausting. The key to dealing with someone like Milton is to accept him for what he is: a penguin who will never fly. Don't take it personally, and don't think you can convince him to change. The sooner we close the gap between our expectations of how Milton might behave and the reality of his nature, the sooner we can detox the conflict.

If you have to work with a Milton (or are related to one), recognize you are dealing with a penguin and stop expecting it to fly. Assume the person you are dealing with is not able to change. Learn to accept him for who he is, limitations and all. Once you've done that, it will be easy to clarify your options and weigh the costs of each one. And the *cost* of continuing to maintain a relationship with a Milton will oftentimes not be in dollars, but in lost peace of mind. Is it worth it to continue this relationship, even if the person is never going to change? If not, maybe it's time to let go.

To determine whether a certain relationship is worth the costs to you, ask yourself some questions about the nature of the relationship. How often do you need to deal with this individual? Is it a lifelong friendship? Is it someone you're forced to work with? Your next-door neighbor? Your mother-in-law? Depending on the nature of the relationship, your tolerance for putting up with the costs will vary. Once you've accepted that the person won't change, you can decide whether the relationship is worth preserving. If so, what are you willing to endure?

HOUSTON, WE HAVE A PENGUIN PROBLEM

Is there anyone in your life who always seems to be doing something that bothers you? Maybe it's your cynical coworker rolling her eyes in that *annoying* way. Maybe it's your boss "asking" you to pick up another shift over the weekend (but really it's a command, not a question). It might be your friend who is always trying to extract a little extra benefit for himself in every exchange with another human being. In any event, if someone is frequently getting under your skin in the same way, it's usually a sign that the two of you are caught in an unhealthy pattern.

It sounds like you've got a penguin problem.

Julie is someone I've known since we were kids, and she had a major penguin problem. She and her ex-husband, John, went through a difficult divorce. She says they had a tense relationship from very early on in their marriage. Money was a big point of contention between them. They didn't struggle financially, but every conversation they had about money followed the same pattern: John would tense up and speak in an agitated, accusatory tone. That triggered anxiety in Julie, and she invariably would find that she was defending herself, oftentimes not even sure what she was defending against. She told John how his behavior affected her and how he turned every conversation about money into an argument. But he didn't stop. And every time it happened, she resented him. Julie and John were caught in a pattern of toxic conflict.

It made sense for them to get divorced, but they still needed to co-parent their kids, which required ongoing discussions about—you guessed it—money. John refused to try couples' therapy when they were married, and he definitely wasn't willing to do so after the divorce.

Julie once complained to me, "He knows the way he talks to me pisses me off, and he keeps doing it just to get under my skin."

I responded, "It sounds like he gets pretty angry during these conversations too, yes?" She nodded. "Do you think he enjoys getting so mad when he talks to you?" I asked. She thought about it for a bit.

"No," she said, finally. "I'm pretty sure he doesn't like it."

I don't know who first said, "The definition of insanity is doing the same thing over and over again and expecting a different result," but it's a good one.[33] I told Julie I didn't know why John reacts that way in conversations about money, but I did know they'd had hundreds of these conversations, and they always follow the same pattern. I asked what she thought

---

33 I've heard this saying mistakenly attributed to Albert Einstein, but he never said it. Doesn't matter, it makes an important point here.

the chances were that he'd speak to her in the same way the next time they discussed money.

"100 percent," she said.

Then I asked, "Have you considered the possibility that John does not know how to have a civil conversation about money with you?" She looked confused for a minute.

"I don't understand," she said. "What do you mean, he doesn't know *how?*"

I gave her my penguin analogy and told her to stop thinking of this behavior as a conscious choice John was making; he can't help himself. He doesn't want these arguments any more than she does, but they keep happening. He's unwilling to enter therapy to work on the problem. So, Julie has two options. First, she can choose to continue the same pattern of getting angry with John every time he acts in this predictable way. Or she can decide to accept that talking about money in the way she wants is something John is not capable of doing. This penguin is never going to fly.

In fairness to John, this is probably a limitation of the relationship more than a reflection on him as an individual. Certain relationships have limitations (particularly longer relationships with lots of baggage). It's possible John has plenty of civil conversations with other people about money that don't end in arguments. It's possible that Julie and John could have developed a healthier, more productive pattern of communication if they had addressed the issues earlier in their relationship. Or maybe not. We can only speculate about what might have been, but we can be certain about the way things are today. It is clear the two of them are trapped in a toxic pattern of communication, and it is unreasonable for Julie to expect John to change. Julie was dealing with a penguin, and there was no value in getting mad at him because he couldn't fly.

Once Julie accepted that John's behavior was unintentional and resulted from a limitation, she stopped taking it personally. It took some effort to remind herself in the heat of their conversations that it's pointless to get mad at penguins, but the more she worked at it, the less anxiety she felt over time. Eventually, she reached the point where John's behavior no longer triggered anxiety, defensiveness, or anger. Julie has chosen to not react in those ways. This choice has improved her relationship with John, and changed her life.

YES, YOU CAN CHOOSE YOUR EMOTIONS

Most of us believe we cannot control our emotional reactions because they are involuntary, but the truth is that we all have the ability to choose. This doesn't mean we can choose to never feel anger, fear, or anxiety. The first chapter of this book explained how those emotions are part of an instinctive response system that is hard-coded into our DNA. But the lifespan of these instinctive emotions is measured in seconds, not hours or days.

We can't stop the initial flash of emotion in response to an external event, like how we may tense up when we hear someone yelling at us. But what happens next is entirely under our control. If we allow our instinctive response to continue, our attention will narrow as our breathing and heart rate accelerate. We focus on how the other person is always making us feel angry or fearful. We "go" with the emotion and let it drive our response. *That* is a choice.

We can choose not to go with the emotion. We can choose to shift our focus away from that instinctive response. Several of the tactics covered throughout this book are designed to pull us out of an instinctive response and help us gain emotional awareness.

Chapter 3 advised, "If you find yourself feeling the physiological responses to conflict—the hair on the back of your neck standing up or your respiration speeding up—stop. Take a beat. Ask yourself, *Am I falling into one of the Conflict Traps? Is the person I'm dealing with falling into one?*"

Chapter 2 explained how the Shopping List Voice can defuse anger and keep survival emotions at bay.

Chapter 6 explained how labeling emotions makes them more manageable.

Once we learn to disrupt our instinctive fear and anger responses, we gain the power to control our emotions, rather than allowing them to control us. It's not easy to break the cycle, but it *is* possible with practice. And the more we work at it, the easier it gets.

Over the years, many people have vented to me about their coworkers. Venting is a prime example of "going" with an emotion rather than trying to disrupt it. Of course, sometimes people need to vent, and that's fine. But I noticed something interesting during those meetings: one of the most common questions people launched at me while complaining about a coworker was, "Why does she always do that?" While they ask this as a rhetorical question, it is actually a real question with a real answer. And seeking out that answer is very productive.

If you continually feel frustration, anger, or some other toxic emotion in response to someone's behavior, dig into that question. *Why* is the person doing this, really? Do you think she is perpetuating this pattern because she is committed to making your life miserable? If the answer is yes, then go with the advice from Chapter 2 and get as far away from that person as fast as possible. But the vast majority of the time it's safe to assume there is another, deeper reason for the individual's behavior.

She probably isn't being difficult on purpose. The problem might be your expectations of her. You might be expecting her to behave in a way that is beyond her ability. Perhaps you expect her to see something that's beyond her vision, hear something that's beyond her hearing, or develop solutions that are outside of the box she's been trained to think inside of. Maybe the problem is that the two of you have fallen into a well-established—albeit toxic—pattern of communication, and there's too much baggage in the relationship for behaviors to change on their own. If any of these options sounds plausible, you might be getting mad at a penguin because it cannot fly.

ACCEPTANCE

Don't Get Mad at Penguins is a lesson in acceptance. Elisabeth Kübler-Ross's classic book *On Death and Dying* changed the way people view and manage grief.[34] The book is most well-

---

34 New York: Collier Books/Macmillan 1970, c1969. Print. Kübler-Ross, Elisabeth.

known for laying out the five stages of grief: denial, anger, bargaining, sadness, and acceptance. We can apply this framework to virtually any situation where we need to accept a difficult reality, especially when we are caught in a penguin problem.

If you find yourself in a recurring conflict with someone you cannot simply cut from your life, it can be helpful to analyze your relationship through this lens.

Imagine you're having a problem with someone at work, and it seems the two of you are always butting heads. Maybe this person speaks to you in a way that feels judgmental or disrespectful, and perhaps his language is triggering a fight or flight response in you. As we know from Chapter 1, this type of situation is fertile ground for unhealthy conflict. Moving through the five stages of grief can look something like this:

Denial: "He's not going to speak that way to me again."

Anger: "He's doing this again, and he knows I don't like it!"

Bargaining: "If I just bite my tongue, this will be over soon, and it won't happen again (this has a bit of denial in it too)."

Sadness: "He always does this in our conversations and will never change."

Acceptance: "This is simply who he is. He's unable to change under these circumstances. Any hope of change begins with me. I must be the one to do something about it."

Acceptance is where we detox the conflict. We take control in acceptance:

"I can calmly explain to him that his approach makes me angry and is unproductive."

"I can now see his behavior for what it is (and not for what I've been misperceiving). It's the behavior of someone who simply doesn't have the ability to behave differently under the circumstances, not someone who is maliciously attempting to anger me."

Importantly, I'm not advocating that we *judge* others for their shortcomings; I'm suggesting we accept the limitations of the relationship without judgment. We don't want to think to ourselves, *I guess my coworker is a self-centered airhead with no talent or regard for other people's feelings, and I just have to accept that about him.* Remember, judgment is a trap that can escalate conflict in its own right. What we need to practice is nonjudgmental acceptance. We must accept others as they truly are and engage with them from that place. This might mean telling ourselves, *I realize this is just how my coworker communicates. I should accept that about him instead of expecting him to change.*

A mild word of caution. I am not advocating that we default to letting people be sub-standard versions of themselves without letting them know of their shortcomings. When we have valuable feedback that can help people grow, withholding that feedback can be a serious disservice. As long as you give corrective feedback in a helpful, supportive way, it won't do any harm, but there are times when it won't do much good either. On these rare occasions, we will be well served by accepting that we are dealing with a penguin.

The story about Ling in Chapter 5 sets the standard we should strive toward. Despite the horrific things her mother did to her, Ling is free from judgment. Rather, she sees her mother as someone who is severely limited in her ability to make genuine connections, and Ling accepts the limitations of her relationship with her mother.

Whenever you find yourself in a repeating pattern of toxic conflict with someone, it is best to assume this person isn't doing anything *to you*. The world isn't working against you. Stop *choosing* to see it that way. You may be personalizing and internalizing people's actions, but that's a choice. You can also choose to accept these behaviors without emotion or judgment.

It can be challenging to accept the limitations of others when those "others" are our relatives. What can you do when someone in your family always devolves every conversation into hurt feelings and anger? You can't just cut this person out of your life. Does that mean you are stuck in a continuous cycle of toxic conflict? Not if you accept that this person is a penguin and stop taking their behavior personally.

Would you take it personally if you were speaking with a toddler rather than a fully grown adult? Or would you just smile and shake your head because you understand the toddler hasn't developed the ability to deal with this situation in a more productive way yet? Well, we all have some areas in which we are less evolved than others. If you find yourself bumping up against someone's less evolved areas, you don't have to let their behavior bother you. Accept this person for who he or she is, limitations and all. Acceptance is where we take control.

DON'T GET MAD AT PENGUINS BECAUSE THEY CAN'T FLY

Between expectation and reality is a space filled with suffering and conflict. The wider that space becomes, the greater our suffering.

Acceptance: We can reduce conflict by accepting people as they are, limitations and all. Accept people's limitations and don't expect them to do things beyond their abilities, even though you really want them to. Getting frustrated at someone for not miraculously changing to meet your expectations is like getting mad at a penguin because it can't fly.

It's about them, not us: When you find yourself in a repeating pattern of toxic conflict with someone, it's best to assume this person doesn't want to make you angry or frustrate you.

You can choose how you react: We all feel the initial flash of an instinctive emotion in response to an external event, but what happens next is entirely within our control. We can choose to allow our emotions to control us, or we can control our emotions.

CHAPTER 8

Conclusion

Our businesses, families, and personal relationships thrive and prosper when we learn to embrace conflict rather than avoid it. The individuals and organizations who embrace and master conflict will always rise to the top. It's not easy, but it most certainly is a skill that anyone can master when equipped with the right tools. Once we learn to detox our conflicts and navigate challenging situations without becoming a bully, getting too competitive, being overly judgmental, or backing away prematurely, we can leverage sticky situations as opportunities to foster candor and accountability, strengthen relationships, and fuel growth.

What often makes conflict difficult to manage is the existence of four powerful and pervasive Conflict Toxins: anger, fear, ego, and judgment. While these four things are healthy and productive when we maintain them within their optimal ranges, they can also easily get out of balance, and this is when we are pulled into one of the four Conflict Traps. Two of the toxins, anger and fear, often reach toxic levels when our fight-or-flight instinct is triggered. The other two, ego and judgment, are the result of our cultural conditioning from an early age.

The callout boxes at the end of each chapter are great summaries for quick reference, and they are reprinted in the Appendix so you have them all in one place. Use them as you encounter conflict in all aspects of your life. Next time you find yourself or the person you're dealing with falling into a Conflict Trap, take a step back. Focus on taking just one breath and carve out a moment to identify the toxins at play and notice how they're pulling you into the trap. Use the strategies we've covered in this book to bring the toxins back into a healthy range, then revisit the corresponding chapter or callout box after the fact to analyze how the conflict unfolded and what, if anything, you could have done differently. This iterative process will dramatically improve your results with each subsequent encounter.

The tools in the final two chapters are helpful in most situations. Making people feel heard is the first step in any successful conflict resolution. Most people aren't willing to consider your perspective until you've fully understood theirs. One helpful tip is to treat the other person as a valuable resource to help you identify the strengths and weaknesses of your own beliefs. Another powerful approach is to restate their argument better than they could have said it themselves. Once they feel heard, they will be motivated to understand your position and work with you on a resolution. Finally, you can also tell a story about a time when you experienced a similar emotion to what the other individual is describing or experiencing.

In the previous chapter, we looked at what you can do when you find yourself repeatedly falling into the same negative patterns of communication with someone. After these encounters, you might wonder to yourself, *Why does he always act like that?* But in fact, the problem isn't with the other person at all. The problem is with your expectations. We set ourselves up for frustration when we expect someone else to behave in a way that is beyond their capabilities. That's like getting mad at a penguin because it can't fly! If your conversations with someone always seem to end in the same way, maybe it's time to accept the fact that they aren't going to change. This is how that person behaves. Don't keep getting frustrated about it. Just accept the limitations of the relationship and move on.

Stop getting mad at penguins.

You are now equipped with some very effective tools for detoxing conflict and staying out of the Conflict Traps, but you must use these tools at the right times and in the right ways. A hammer is a great tool, but it isn't appropriate for every problem you'll face when building a house. You're going to want some pliers, screwdrivers, wrenches, clamps, and a power saw as well. And you'll need to know when each tool should be used and what the proper technique is for utilizing it. Similarly, this book provides a set of tools for dealing with a wide range of conflicts. Some of these tools are versatile and can be used in many situations, like a hammer. Others are extremely effective in a more limited capacity, like a 1/16" Allen wrench.

We need to understand which of the four Conflict Traps we are facing before we decide how to respond to a particular situation. Once we understand the nature of a conflict and the available tools, the right approach becomes clear. When this happens, it's much easier to engage without triggering toxins in ourselves or in others. We can jump into dicey interpersonal situations while keeping our prehistoric instincts at bay. We'll be able to maintain active neural pathways to our prefrontal cortex, which allow us to maintain our reasoning faculties, our ability to consider multiple perspectives, and our problem-solving capacity, even as tensions escalate. Most of us don't view conflict in these terms, so we never take the time to work on it. But with this perspective and some practice, the art of conflict is something everyone can master. It is surprisingly easy once we understand the causes of toxic conflict and gain some tools to detox it and leverage it for good.

BECOME AN AMBASSADOR OF HEALTHY CONFLICT

Ambassador: a person who acts as a representative or promoter of a specified activity.

My greatest hope for anyone who reads this book—that means you, my friend—is that you not only embrace healthy conflict in your own dealings, but that you feel empowered as an ambassador of healthy conflict to the rest of the world. This isn't some holier-than-thou delusion of grandeur. The simple truth is that we all witness others engaging in conflict every day. We may not be able to do much about conflicts playing out on TV or social media, but we can declare our immediate sphere of influence as a zone free of toxic conflict. We can humbly require that anyone who enters our sphere eliminate toxins from their interactions. If you find a particular tool works well for you, share it with others. Let it be known that anyone who enters your sphere will engage in genuine, meaningful, productive relationships that enjoy all the benefits of healthy conflict. Spread the gospel. The more people who recognize the value of embracing healthy conflict, the better the world will be.

APPENDIX

Chapter Callout Boxes

Chapter 1: To Embrace or Resist Conflict

Embrace conflict
Healthy conflict propels people and organizations forward. Toxic conflict slows us down and causes pain.

Understand the roots
All conflict follows a set of simple, predictable patterns. There are two main reasons why engaging in healthy conflict is difficult for most people: the way our brains are wired, and the way we are raised.

- **Nature:** Our survival instincts have been bred over billions of years and are hard coded into our DNA. We have a natural fight-or-flight system that is automatically activated in response to conflict.
- **Nurture:** We are socialized from a young age with conflicting messages on how to manage conflict. We are taught to judge others while simultaneously viewing judgment as impolite; be open and honest with others, but to stay quiet if we don't have something nice to say. These conflicting messages are confusing.

The Conflict Toxins

Our nature and nurture produce four factors which are useful and productive when they stay in optimal ranges, but which become toxic when they fall below or rise above those optimal ranges. They are responsible for most unhealthy conflict.

- **Fear**
- **Anger**
- **Judgment**
- **Ego**

The Conflict Traps

There are four common traps we can be pulled into when toxins build in a conflict:

- **Bully Trap**
- **Need-to-Win Trap**
- **Avoidance Trap**
- **Judgment Trap**

Chapter 2: The Bully Trap

UNDERSTANDING THE BULLY TRAP

Not all bullying is a trap
The Bully Trap refers to situations in which toxic anger, fear, or ego drive bullying behavior with the unintended consequence of making conflict worse, or creating toxic conflict where none existed.

The Bully
Trap occurs in high-stress scenarios: When our emotions are raw and the pressure is on, these are optimal conditions for feelings of anger, fear, and ego to elevate to toxic levels. This drives behavior that can unintentionally trigger someone else's fight-or-flight response.

Three factors that feed toxins
These factors often lead to toxic anger, fear, and ego, pulling us into the Bully Trap.

- **Authority:** Even compassionate people can fall into the Bully Trap when in a position of authority. In positions of power, we adopt a more ego-centric perspective, making us less considerate and more likely to bully others.
- **Passion:** Sometimes we can be seen as a bully in someone else's eyes because we are passionate, and our excitement comes off as aggression.
- **Depersonalization:** When we view others solely based on the roles they play in our lives, we're susceptible to the Bully Trap.

The Bully Trap does significant damage
Bullying shuts down communication. In the workplace, this promotes undermining, manipulation, and more bullying. It takes energy away from positive growth. Bullying destroys otherwise productive feedback.

TOOLS TO OVERCOME THE BULLY TRAP

Shopping List Voice
Detox communication by speaking in a matter-of-fact, dispassionate tone, like you are telling your friend what you'd like them to pick up for you at the store.

No venting
Never use feedback to beat up on somebody (that is a sign of weakness, not strength). Process anger before giving feedback. Control your emotions; don't allow them to control you.

Reaffirm
When delivering harsh feedback, take the opportunity to reaffirm the person.

Clarify
Clarify the goal of message before you deliver it. This neutralizes toxins and tightens up communication.

Humanize the other person
Before confronting someone, spend a few minutes thinking about things you have in common.

Responding to a bully
All of the above are just as effective when on the receiving end of the Bully Trap.

Chapter 3: The Need-to-Win Trap

UNDERSTANDING THE NEED-TO-WIN TRAP

Winning can be a distraction
When your desire to beat someone else causes you to lose sight of your larger goal, you have fallen into the Need-to-Win Trap.

Emotion can be a weakness
We often rely on feelings of anger or self-righteousness to build ourselves up into feeling powerful but, in fact, these emotions can be our greatest weaknesses.

Two Toxins that Lead to the Need-to-Win Trap:
- **Ego:** The need to feed our ego can cause us to fight harder and longer even when doing so no longer serves our larger goal. Reaching a compromise with someone else can feel like losing or weakness, so our ego pushes us to win, not settle. The other person's ego can drive them in the same way.
- **Overinvestment:** We have a harder time giving something up after we've invested is the is the Sunk Cost Fallacy, which describes ourdesire to continue pursuing a goal to recoup our investment even when doing so is no longer in our best interest.

TOOLS TO OVERCOME THE NEED-TO-WIN TRAP

Notice the signs

Learn to be aware of when your need to win is being triggered so you can stop yourself from getting pulled into the trap.

Catering to your own ego is costly, but catering to someone else's is free

When you feel the physiological effects of conflict, ask yourself: *Is my ego driving my behavior? Is the other person's ego driving their behavior?*

- If your ego is driving the conflict, hit the pause button. Make an intellectual decision as to whether you want to continue; don't let your ego drive your behavior.
- If you see that the other person's ego is driving the conflict, feed that person's ego. It will cost you nothing.

Cut your losses on overinvestment

When you find yourself pursuing a goal because you've already invested so much, it is easy to assess whether overinvestment is driving your need to win. If so, cut your losses.

Accept the nature of a Milton

If you're dealing with someone who needs to win all the time, don't get pulled into the trap for the sake of competition. Instead, accept that the person will not change, clarify your options, and select the one that costs the least.

Chapter 4: The Avoidance Trap

UNDERSTANDING THE AVOIDANCE TRAP

Avoiding conflict makes it worse

In the short term, it may feel safer to avoid a conflict, but that allows the issue to fester and grow. Toxic fear causes us to run from conflict rather than embrace it for success. Most people will run away from a small conflict that is immediate, even if it sends us running toward a larger conflict that's not immediate.

Three sources of toxic fear that lead to the Avoidance Trap:

- **Lack of Psychological Safety:** Fear of being punished or humiliated for raising a concern or calling out a mistake.
- **Impression Management:** Fear that speaking up will put us in a negative light.
- **Socialization:** Fear that offering constructive criticism will come across as disrespectful, disagreeable, or impolite.

TOOLS TO OVERCOME THE AVOIDANCE TRAP

Make the initiation of conflict a job requirement
Regularly schedule debrief and pre-brief meetings in which people aren't doing their job if they remain silent. Benefits:

- Provide recurring opportunities to uncover problems, so that bad news surfaces faster.
- Create a psychologically safe environment that frees people from the social stigma of initiating conflict.
- Motivate and empower people to continually seek improvement.

It's a learning exercise, not an execution problem
Stress the importance of hearing everyone's unique perspective to get the broadest view possible.

Build a culture of candor and accountability
Encourage candid feedback, view mistakes as opportunities for learning and improvement (not badges of shame), and honor those who hold themselves accountable.

Make it a habit
Weekly reporting from each team member with commitments for the upcoming week and performance against last week's commitments.

Be a model
Regularly hold yourself accountable for your own mistakes.

Run toward conflict
Seek out conflicts as opportunities to demonstrate character, build trust, and strengthen relationships.

Chapter 5: The Judgment Trap

UNDERSTANDING THE JUDGMENT TRAP

Not all judgment leads to a trap

Judgment can be a valuable tool that informs our decisions. But when judgment mixes with toxins like fear, anger, self-righteousness, or resentment, the resulting cocktail is a form of toxic judgment that distracts us from our goals and creates unhealthy conflict.

Judging is a natural impulse

Our judgmental instincts were lifesaving for our ancestors, who had to make quick decisions based on very little information. Today we no longer face life-or-death situations, but our brains are still wired to react like our ancestors' did in response to saber-toothed tigers.

The consequences of toxic judgment:

- **Prevents us from working with others:** When our judgments stop us from working with someone, even though that person can serve our larger objective, the Judgment Trap has prevented us from accomplishing our goals.
- **Communication triggers negative responses:** Our judgment of someone can come across in our tone of voice and choice of words, causing them to get defensive, resentful, and angry.
- **Consumes time and energy:** Even if someone is deserving of our judgment, holding onto judgment weighs us down and consumes valuable time and energy that could be going towards achieving our goals.

TOOLS TO OVERCOME THE JUDGMENT TRAP

Use judgment from others as an opportunity to learn
Being judged never feels good, but sometimes we need to feel judged in order to recognize our shortcomings so that we can improve.

Communicate without judgment
Focus on describing rather than evaluating. It is possible for us to feel judgment and still choose non-judgmental words.

Use it then lose it
Judgment is useful if it protects us from harm or progresses us towards our larger goal, but as soon as our judgment stops doing those things, it is more productive to let it go.

Chapter 6: Making People Feel Heard

**UNDERSTANDING THE IMPORTANCE AND
DIFFICULTY OF MAKING OTHERS FEEL HEARD**

Making people feel heard is a critical step in resolving conflict
Most people will not be willing to consider other perspectives until they feel their perspective is fully understood. We can move conflicts toward resolution by understanding others.

Confirmation bias is a significant obstacle
Our emotional attachments to our pre-existing beliefs make our arguments weaker, not stronger. Only after we learn the strengths of other opinions and the weaknesses of our own ideas are we equipped to convince others we understand them so that we can resolve a conflict.

Genuine curiosity promotes genuine listening, and genuine listening promotes genuine understanding

TOOLS FOR OVERCOMING CONFIRMATION BIAS AND MAKING OTHERS FEEL HEARD

Acknowledge confirmation bias has power
When we are consciously aware of confirmation bias, we have more control over our reactions.

Seek information that disproves your position
View the other person as a valuable resource to learn about the strengths and weaknesses in your position.

State the other person's position better than they said it themselves
When someone articulates your position better than you can, you feel understood. The sooner you can do that for someone else, the more motivated they will be to understand your position and work toward a resolution, and the more energy you'll have between you to do it.

Relate your understanding on an emotional level
Share a story of a time when you felt how the other person feels now, to demonstrate genuine understanding.

ORDER OF OPERATIONS FOR CONFLICT RESOLUTION

1) Understand the conflict by listening. Overcome confirmation bias by:
   a) acknowledging its power, and
   b) seeking out information that disproves previous way of thinking.

2) Communicate your understanding of the other side's position so they feel heard:
   a) state their position better than they said it themselves, and
   b) relate your understanding on an emotional level.

3) Work on a resolution.

Chapter 7: Don't Get Mad at Penguins Because They Can't Fly

DON'T GET MAD AT PENGUINS BECAUSE THEY CAN'T FLY

Between expectation and reality is a space filled with suffering and conflict.
The wider that space becomes, the greater our suffering.

Acceptance: We can reduce conflict by accepting people as they are, limitations and all.
Accept people's limitations and don't expect them to do things beyond their abilities, even though you really want them to. Getting frustrated at someone for not miraculously changing to meet your expectations is like getting mad at a penguin because it can't fly.

It's about them, not us.
When you find yourself in a repeating pattern of toxic conflict with someone, it's best to assume this person doesn't want to make you angry or frustrate you.

You can choose how you react
We all feel the initial flash of an instinctive emotion in response to an external event, but what happens next is entirely within our control. We can choose to allow our emotions to control us, or we can control our emotions.

ACKNOWLEDGMENTS

I am sure there are authors out there who create awe-inspiring works of literature by simply channeling wisdom from their brilliant minds onto pages of written text. I am not one of them. Writing this book was a team effort. I am truly blessed to have the support, friendship, and guidance of so many remarkable people. I owe them immeasurable gratitude.

This book wouldn't have been possible without my parents, who not only gave me life (can't really top that) but whose unconditional love, encouragement, and support have been meaningful beyond words. My first real lessons in engaging healthy conflict were watching my dad interact with others, first through the eyes of a child and then as lawyer in the practice of law together. He never shied away from conflict and he had a remarkable ability to relate to people from all walks of life, regardless of race, wealth, religion, you name it. The more different someone was from him, the more he wanted to understand their background and perspective. Dad, it's been fifteen years since you passed away and not a day has gone by when I haven't thought about you. I so very much wish you could have been involved in writing this book—you would've loved every minute of it. And of course, my mom, who played a very active role in this book, spending countless hours as a test reader, researcher, editor, sounding board, and cheer-leader. Your perspective and feedback most definitely widened the audience of this book. Mom, it was such a joy sharing this process with you. At eighty-four years old as of the book's publication date (sorry to share your age with everyone), your intellectual curiosity and analysis is as sharp as it's ever been. Far more than that, words cannot express how grateful I am for everything you are and do. I love you, Mom.

There are several people worthy of special mention. To Eric Lefkofsky, who gave me the idea to write this book, who supported me every step of the way, and who continued to pressure me until it was done—I cherish our lifelong friend-ship. To Andy Earle, you guided me through the entire pro-cess, teaching me how to write a book, influencing everything from the book's structure to the flow of ideas and concepts, to the placement of chapters, paragraphs, and individual sen-tences. Without you, it would have taken me twice as long to write a book that wouldn't have been even a third as good. To Josh Linkner, you were instrumental in helping me craft the keynote speech on conflict that was the original source mate-rial for this book. In addition to being one of my test read-ers, your generosity in sharing lessons from your own book writing success (including two *New York Times* bestsellers) has been invaluable to me in this process, especially your intro-duction of me to Post Hill Press. And to the folks at Post Hill Press, who decided in their infinite wisdom to actually pub-lish this book, thank you! To Paulius Maciulevicius, whom I met on a two day hike up and down a volcano in Guatemala listening to many of the lessons in these pages, thank you for insisting that I change the title of this book from *The Conflict Cleanse* to *Don't Get Mad at Penguins*—it's a much better title.

As this book came to life, I enlisted some of the smartest and insightful people I know to be test readers. They read through the rough manuscript chapter by chapter (and some of them read multiple versions of chapters). The published version of this book is waaayyy better because of their feedback. To my test readers, I am deeply appreciative of your gracious generosity with not only your time and expertise, but a genuine desire to help make this book a valuable resource that can truly change people's lives for the better (in alphabetical order): Ian Burnstein, Matt Egrin, John Feldman, Marlene Karp, Joe Lash, Josh Linkner, Robb Lippitt, Sagar Parvataneni, Ira Schlussel, Cory Tincher, and Lee Trepeck. You all are extremely busy people so your contribution means a great deal.

And finally, writing this book would not have been possible without the unwavering support of my wonderful and amazing family, including my wife, Rachel; and daughters, Jillian, Amelia, and Violet. Rach, thank you for reading multiple rough drafts and giving me several points of critical feedback that made this book better and, more importantly, for being the best partner in life anyone could hope for. To all four of you, thank you for your excitement and encouragement for this project. Most importantly, thank you for being the beautiful souls that enrich my life day in and day out. Your happiness is everything to me.